Getting the Most From Your

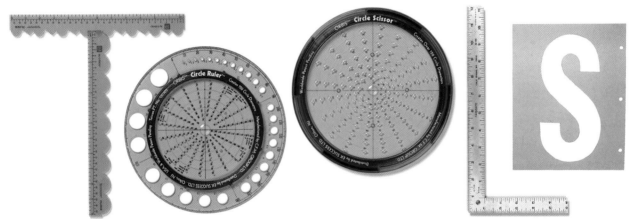

D1456093

MEMORY
MAKERS
BOOKS

Executive Editor Kerry Arquette   Founder Michele Gerbrandt

Art Director Andrea Zocchi
Designer Nick Nyffeler
Craft Editor Jodi Amidei
Art Acquisitions Editor Janetta Wieneke
Photographer Ken Trujillo
Contributing Photographers Marc Creedon, Brenda Martinez
Contributing Writer Torrey Miller
Editorial Support Emily Curry Hitchingham, MaryJo Regier, Dena Twinem
Hand Model Ann Kitayama
Contributing 2003 Memory Makers Masters Valerie Barton, Brandi Ginn, Torrey Miller, Kelli Noto, Heidi Schueller, Holle Wiktorek

Memory Makers® Getting the Most From Your Scrapbook Tools

Published by Memory Makers Books, an imprint of F & W Publications, Inc.
12365 Huron Street, Suite 500, Denver, CO 80234
Phone 1-800-254-9124
First edition. Printed in Singapore.
07 06 05 04 03 5 4 3 2 1

Library of Congress Cataloging-in-Publication Data

Getting the most from your scrapbook tools.-- 1st ed.
    p. cm.
    Includes bibliographical references and index.
    ISBN 1-892127-19-9
    1. Photographs--Conversation and restoration. 2. Photograph albums--Equipment and supplies. 3. Scrapbooks--Equipment and supplies. I. Memory Makers Books.

    TR465.G485 2003
    745.593--dc22
                                                                2003059669

Distributed to trade and art markets by
F & W Publications, Inc.
4700 East Galbraith Road, Cincinnati, OH 45236
Phone 1-800-289-0963

Memory Makers Books is the home of Memory Makers, the scrapbook magazine dedicated to educating and inspiring scrapbookers. To subscribe, or for more information, call 1-800-366-6465.
Visit us on the Internet at www.memorymakersmagazine.com

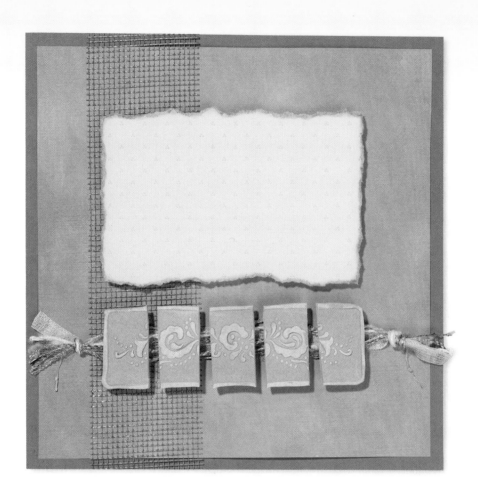

Special thanks to the manufacturers of scrapbook tools who have contributed their products and their talents to create this book. Also thanks to the artists who stretched their imaginations and dreamed up the original techniques and scrapbook pages featured in this book.

Table of Contents

12 Cutting Tools

From craft knives to paper trimmers, cutting tools are the meat and potatoes of scrapbook tools. These indispensable supplies allow the scrapbooker to consistently make straight cuts with ease and accuracy, creating precise borders, mats and other page elements. Decorative scissors turn cuts into eye-pleasing patterns that add something special to page elements such as journaling blocks and titles or embellishments.

40 Shape Cutters, Punches, Die Cuts

There is no easier way to make perfect circles and basic shapes than by using shape and circle cutters, punches and die cuts. Most scrapbookers have an ample supply of these nifty tools on hand, or have ready access to a selection through their local scrapbook or hobby store. These specialized tools make it possible for a scrapbooker to repeatedly carve the same shape multiple times to form creative and consistent borders, embellishments, corners and other page elements.

66 Stencils, Templates, Decorative Rulers

Considered a luxury to some scrapbookers, these tools have become indispensible to others. Lettering templates allow scrapbookers to design and create beautiful titles. Shape templates and stencils can be the answer to many embellishment challenges. Decorative rulers help artists coax straight edges into pretty patterns. All of these versatile tools allow the scrapbooker to create complex designs with finesse.

Rain

Even the rain couldn't dampen our spirits or spoil our mood on this glorious day at Discovery Cove.
Daniel, Anna and Sasha
Florida - 2001

Introduction

If you're like me, over time you have accumulated an extensive and sophisticated array of scrapbook tools. There is just something about purchasing the latest tool that whets the creative appetite, inspiring us simply by its "newness" and promise to perform its given function. And yet, as wonderful as they are, investing in scrapbook tools can take a substantial bite out of any budget and so it behooves us to get as much bang for our buck as possible from those that we already own. Finding innovative ways to use scrapbook tools can be a satisfying process of experimentation and discovery. After all, at the very foundation of creativity is resourcefulness.

Getting the Most From Your Scrapbook Tools was created to help jump-start your imagination and inspire you to think of new ways to use the tools that are currently part of your scrapbook arsenal. Along with an idea gallery full of great layouts, you'll find a wide range of innovative techniques that can be used for numerous page themes.

The art you'll see inside *Getting the Most From Your Scrapbook Tools* came from a number of sources. In an effort to provide you with the most comprehensive sampling of fresh ideas, we challenged tool manufacturers and professional scrapbookers to submit cutting-edge concepts. We also held a contest and encouraged readers like you to send us pages displaying new tool usage. The result? This terrific volume featuring ways to use stencils to create stamps, templates to produce polymer clay page accents, cutting tools to craft unique paper art, and much more.

We thank those artists and manufacturers who accepted the challenge and submitted concepts for this book—those whose pages are included as well as those whose work does not appear due to space limitations. Now the challenge is put to you. Get set to explore and most of all have fun!

Michele

Michele Gerbrandt
Founding Editor
Memory Makers magazine

Basic Tools Every Scrapbooker Needs

As the scrapbooking phenomenon has grown, so has the outcry for more and better tools. Manufacturers have stepped up to the plate to provide a seemingly endless parade of tools to make scrapbooking easier and more enjoyable. In this book, we've focused on the most popular and most basic tools available to scrapbookers today— those found in most scrapbookers' workboxes. These are the tools used by artists to create the spectacular scrapbook pages featured in this book.

Trimmer

Today's trimmers are updated versions of the old guillotine-type paper cutters we remember from school. These modern renditions are compact, safe and far more affordable. They are a convenient way to quickly cut straight lines.

Craft Knife

Craft knives have been in office supply and hardware stores forever. They've finally found their niche in scrapbooking. Craft knives offer the scrapbooker a means to create highly detailed cuts with ease. They have inexpensive disposable blades which ensure effortless, clean cuts every time.

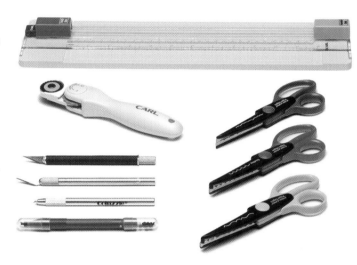

Decorative Scissors

For years Mother's pinking shears were the only decorative-edge scissors available. Not anymore. Now the patterns on the market are endless, including deckle, scallop, stamp-edge and fancy Victorian designs. These creative cutting tools are a welcome addition to the scrapbooking family.

Decorative Rulers

Gone are the days when straight-edge rulers dominated the scene. Decorative rulers have made the move from the drafting table to the scrapbooking table. We are no longer just limited to cumbersome French curves either. Decorative rulers are available in a variety of styles including wavy, scalloped Victorian and Grecian key designs. The choices are boundless.

Templates and Stencils

Templates help create perfect circles and ovals as well as other distinct shapes. Some come with cutting tools, allowing scrapbookers to skip the tedium of tracing prior to cutting, by performing the tasks consecutively. Stencils, including brass stencils, provide complex designs and patterns to add that finishing touch to scrapbook spreads.

Shape Cutters

Shape cutters such as circle, oval and nested-template cutting systems make it possible for scrapbookers to make clean and precise cuts every time. Durable and inexpensive, these tools are available from many major manufacturers and various systems provide unique results.

Punches

Who would have guessed that the humble beginnings of the punch craze started in an office supply store with a single hole punch? Punches have become a major staple in scrapbookers' tool collections. Just when we think we've seen all the designs there can be, here comes a whole new line of must-have punches in sizes from tiny to jumbo. There's a punch for just about every scrapbooking need.

Die cuts

Like paper trimmers, these paper cutters have also found life beyond the classroom. From their modest beginnings as tools used to create bulletin board decor, die cuts have evolved into multifaceted phenomena. Whatever the image you are seeking for your scrapbook page, you can bet you will find it immortalized in die-cut form. Simple die-cut shapes can be customized with colorful embellishments that add dimension and pizazz.

Beyond the Basics:

Other great tools to add to your scrapbook toolbox

- Adhesive application machine: a tool that adds an adhesive backing to flat objects
- Paper crimpers: create three dimensional wavy ridges and designs in paper
- Wire tools: round nose pliers, wire cutters, peg boards, coiling rods
- Rubber stamps: create simple and complex stamped designs
- Heat gun: makes ink and other materials dry more quickly and aids embossing
- Eyelet setting tools: punch tiny holes anywhere
- Piercing tools: create holes for stitching or creating patterns
- Styluses: used to impress a design into paper, metal or other surfaces
- Button shank removers: allow easy removal of shanks so buttons can lay flat against a page

Care and Storage of Tools

How many times have you sat down to scrapbook only to find yourself spending more time and energy locating the right tools than actually creating layouts? One of the keys to enjoyable and productive scrapbooking is having your tools both accessible and in great working condition. Follow our tips for organizing, storing and caring for your tools and your scrapbooking time and money will be well spent.

Decorative Scissors

Over time decorative scissors can become dull. Some say you can sharpen them by cutting through heavy foil. Gently file down any rough spots along the pattern teeth to ensure smooth cutting. Check with the manufacturer before adding lubrication which may damage the plastic hinges and housings of decorative scissors. Store scissors by hanging them on a pegboard or expandable wooden coat rack. Sort them by pattern and tuck them away in a plastic tub. Stand them on end in a partitioned plastic Lazy Susan or wooden box. Keep them holstered in the elastic loops of a cropping bag. Place them in the compartments of an over-the-door hanging shoe rack. Do not expose scissors to high heat or humidity.

Paper Trimmers

Blades can become dull with repeated use. Be sure to keep extra blades on hand and change them frequently. If your trimmer is creating crooked cuts, contact the manufacturer. Many offer limited lifetime warranties on the trimmer's parts and provide repair or replacement at no charge. Store trimmers flat. Do not expose them to high heat as this may cause warping.

Craft Knives

Craft knives can become sticky with adhesive. Clean them with a product intended to remove adhesives and glues. Lost lids can be replaced with small pieces of clear plastic tubing from the hardware store, or with discarded marker lids. Some artists plunge their craft knives, blade first, into an eraser for storing, although this may dull the blade. Replace the blade often and discard used blades carefully.

Templates, Stencils, Shape Cutters

Templates are delicate and can easily be damaged either with a cutting tool or by catching upon one another. To minimize damage, do not use a craft knife against the edges of the template or stencil. Instead, trace the pattern with a pen or pencil, remove the template or stencil and then cut the design out of the paper. Sort plastic lettering templates by category and store them out of direct sunlight in page protectors within three-ring notebooks. By placing a piece of dark paper between each stencil/template in the notebook, it is much easier to see patterns. Place brass stencils in the sleeves of a 4 x 6" photo album. File heavier templates in hanging folders or zippered plastic bags.

Decorative Rulers

Decorative rulers can become dirty with ink, lead and adhesive which can transfer to your next project. Clean off all pen/pencil marks and adhesive after each use. If possible, store rulers flat, as storing on edge or standing up will cause warping. You may wish to punch a hole on the end of rulers and place them on a metal ring or hang them from a pegboard. Consider storing rulers in partitioned sheet protectors made for long border stickers and place them in three-ring notebooks. Avoid high heat and direct sunlight to prevent warping. Always trace your pattern and cut by hand. Avoid using decorative edges as direct cutting guides for your craft knife, as the edge can be easily nicked and sliced.

Punches

Clean adhesive from punches with a commercial adhesive remover. Sharpen dull punches by cutting through heavy foil. Gently file down any rough spots along the pattern to ensure smooth cutting. Keep them from sticking by punching through waxed paper. Punches can be taken apart relatively easily for internal lubrication with a lubricating spray (check with manufacturer first). Store punches by category in labeled plastic tubs or in an over-the-door organizing system specifically designed for punches. Stow them in the plastic compartments of a cropping bag, in the pockets of a hanging plastic shoe organizer or in labeled drawers of a plastic multi-drawer chest. Make skinny punch shelves from 2 x 2" pieces of wood. Do not expose punches to high heat.

Die Cuts

When die cuts become dull, sharpening should be done by the manufacturer or the manufacturer's agent. Contact the manufacturer about replacing damaged rubber matting as well. Before storing dies, remove all stray bits of paper from the die surface. Categorize dies and store dies flat, if possible, away from high heat or direct sunlight. Dies can be stored in much the same fashion as punches.

Cutting Tools

In construction, you start building from the ground up. In cooking, you make the cake before you frost it. It's only logical. Scrapbooking is no different. That's why so many scrapbookers invest first in cutting tools such as paper trimmers, craft knives and decorative scissors. These are the foundation blocks of scrapbook equipment. While familiarity with these tools by no means breeds contempt, it can result in many scrapbookers overlooking and underestimating the value of these tools. They reach for them only to trim paper to size and cut photo mats. However these toolbox staples hold a wealth of possibilities and potential. With some imagination, you can utilize cutting tools to create unique decorative accents for your layouts. This chapter presents some interesting techniques that will help you view cutting tools from a different angle.

Valerie Barton, Flowood, Mississippi

Scootin' Along

Use a paper trimmer to create a border that meanders around the page like a complex sidewalk that just calls for a scooter ride (see adjacent page for border instructions). Place pictures on background. Enfold photos with border strips. Embellish with tiny mirrors and eyelets. Attach the vellum journaling block to the page with eyelets. Make the "Scootin'" title by embellishing a metal-rimmed tag with stickers, fibers, tiny mirrors and a ball chain. Attach a metal nameplate with decorative brads.

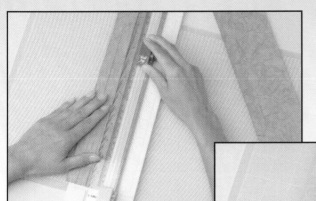

ONE To create the sidewalk border seen on the Scootin' Along page (left), cut a 3 x 12" double-sided mulberry strip. (Double-sided cardstock or patterned paper can also be used.) Use a paper trimmer to make parallel cuts along the length of the paper strip. Space the slices ½" apart. Leave 1" at the bottom of the strip uncut to hold section together.

TWO Randomly fold cut paper strips to form the desired design. Adhere the folded pattern to the page.

Valerie Barton, Flowood, Mississippi

Girls Just Wanna Have Fun

For a funky variation on the method shown above, use double-sided patterned paper strips and torn vellum to create a title. Adhere your title to a patterned paper background. Tear cardstock into a photo mat and chalk the torn edges; embellish with fibers, 3-D vellum flower stickers and buttons. Add metal-rimmed vellum tags for journaling. Place a small piece of the title paper behind each tag. Secure tags to page with decorative brads. Finish the page with a torn vellum tag accent. Chalk torn edges and tie with fiber.

Ruth Anne Oliver, Lafayette, Colorado

Wild Wild West

No need to cut perfect rectangles and squares for this rootin' tootin' layout! Choose five contrasting or coordinating colors of cardstock. Select one color for the background and four colors to be used for the embellishments. Use a paper trimmer to cut random, asymmetric four-sided shapes from those papers selected for the embellishments (see instructions on adjacent page). Mat photos using asymmetric shapes as well. Create the journaling block and title by either hand lettering or stamping. Add penwork to journaling block, title, mats and embellishments and mount to page.

Alone We Can Do So Little…

Use the paper-slicing technique seen in Wild Wild West (left), to create this unique border. Use a paper trimmer to cut a 3 x 10" strip of cardstock into asymmetric pieces. Reassemble the cut pieces on background paper, replacing just one piece of the cut border strip with a block of contrasting colored cardstock. Adhere the cut pieces to the background leaving small gaps between blocks. Mat small photos off-center on colored blocks; adhere to border strip. Double mat the focal photo. Cut a 2 x 2" piece of colored cardstock for the journaling block. Mount cut pieces along another strip of asymmetrically cut cardstock. Journal.

Ruth Anne Oliver,
Lafayette, Colorado
Photos, Tracy Trulove Young,
Meadow Sweet Studio

ONE To create the asymmetrical page elements seen on the Wild Wild West spread (left), place cardstock in trimmer at an angle and smoothly cut into four-sided shapes. Vary your angle and size of paper blocks for more visual appeal.

Great Sense of Humor **Loving** *Patient* **Kind**

Even Tempered **Honest** Stress Manager

Resilient Peace Maker **SECURE** Sensitive

Kim Morelli, Coral Springs, Florida

Daniel Ryan

This unique all-boy page was made using parts of a Fiskar's personal trimmer that some people don't even know exist! Begin by printing the title text onto vellum. Tear the vellum to size by sliding it under the trimmer's cutting guide. Use the guide's edge to tear the vellum. Fashion the dimensional pleat accent by using the trimmer's scoring blade and cutting blade (see instructions on adjacent page). Adhere the pleat to the page and fasten the title over the pleat with decorative brads. Complete the page by hand journaling in varied fonts and add leaf laser die cut in corner for final embellishment.

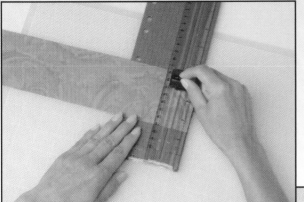

ONE To create the dimensional pleat accent seen on the Daniel Ryan page (left), cut patterned paper into three 3 x 12" strips. Use a scoring blade to score across the width of the strips. Begin the first score 1" from the end of the paper strip. The following score will be ½" from the primary score. Continue to work down the strip alternating between 1" and ½" scores. Repeat the process with three 2 x 12" strips of contrasting patterned paper.

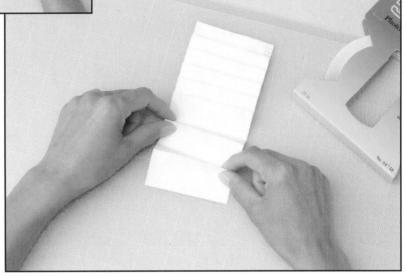

TWO Accordion-fold the paper strips along the score lines. Lay the folded strips end-to-end, pattern-side down on a work surface. Overlap the ends slightly. Apply adhesive tape lengthwise to the strips to secure all three strips together and to hold the folds. Repeat the process in assembling three strips of 2 x 12" contrasting patterned paper to create the layered border effect.

Hula-Little Grass Shack

You can almost feel warm breezes wafting across this tropical layout which utilizes a paper trimmer to create the swaying fringe. For grass-skirt accents, make tiny parallel cuts into 1" wide strips of cardstock. Do not allow cuts to completely sever the strip (leave a ⅛" border along one edge uncut). Use a lettering template and craft knife to cut cardstock letters for the title. Sprinkle with clear embossing powder for texture. Complete by gently daubing a dark green ink pad along the edges of the letters and the mat of the focal picture; add stamps to the title. Create floral lei accents by loosely stringing punched flowers across page.

Brandi Ginn, Lafayette, Colorado
Photos, Donald Bryant Sr., Aurora, Colorado

It's hard to convince people that this is a real, live alligator, but trust me...it is! His name is Scarface and those are really my hands in his mouth. He was 10 feet 8 inches long and weighed about 500 pounds. Tom found this tacky little tourist spot outside of Alamosa, CO and had to take us there on our trip to the Sand Dunes. At first Haley and I had no intentions of sitting on one, but as more and more people stepped up and did it, I couldn't resist taking this chance. I mean, when else in my life will I be able to touch a live alligator, let alone sit on one.

Scarface

Jodi Amidei, Memory Makers

Scarface

It takes little courage, but some know-how, to create this striking page. Make the realistic-looking 3-D border from the background paper using a paper trimmer or craft knife and foam dots (see instructions on adjacent page). Double mat photos. Print journaling on vellum and tear edges. Add chalk to torn vellum edges. Tear and chalk vellum backdrop for the title and add letter stickers. Mat the entire page on cardstock.

ONE To create the alligator border seen on the Scarface page (left), fold back a 2" strip along the left side of the background paper. Right sides will be together. Draw a line lengthwise, 1" from the creased edge. Make pencil marks every 1" along the drawn line, beginning 1½" from the top of the page. Create another set of pencil marks every 1" along the folded edge of the paper. This set of marks should begin at the top of the page. Connect pencil marks on the crease with marks on the line, creating diagonal lines. Cut along the diagonal lines with a paper trimmer or craft knife.

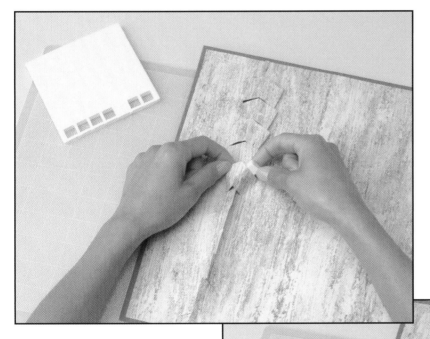

TWO Open the folded sheet of paper and turn it pattern-side up. Place hand on either side of the sheet of paper and gently push toward the paper's center. This will create a "peak" along the previously creased section. Adhere the paper to a piece of cardstock background in this "peaked" position. Place self adhesive foam spacers under each V-shaped section of the peak. Gently push down each peaked section to adhere it to the background.

THREE Lightly chalk the edges of each raised, "scale" platform with both green and brown chalk to create dimension.

My father doesn't tell me how to live; he lives, and lets me watch him do it. *Adapted from Clarence Budington Kelland*

D a d

H e r o

Trying to describe my love for my father is not easy. Words that convey my admiration of him just don't come without effort. He has had such an influence and impact on my life. I know that he shaped who I was as a child, but more noticeable to me now is how he still guides me as an adult – not by telling me how to live, but by setting an example of the type of person I still strive to become. His integrity, compassion, sincerity, and virtues will always seem out of reach for me, but they will continue to give me something to aspire towards in my own life.

FATHER

Jodi Amidei, Memory Makers

Father

This beautiful border, created using a technique similar to that featured on the Scarface layout (page 20), can add dimension and drama to just about any layout. Make two border sections (see illustrations below). Place the first border section on a strip of torn patterned paper. Place a second border section on the strip so that it precisely mirrors the previously positioned border section. You may need to flip one strip over to get the pattern to work. Embellish the page with metal letters. Affix journaling and quotation blocks with decorative brads. Mat photo and adhere with metal photo corners. Embellish with fiber.

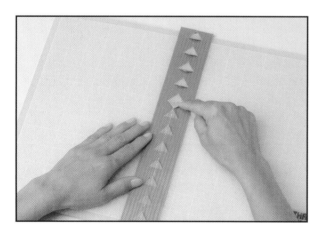

ONE Cut two 2 x 12" strips of double-sided patterned paper. Fold the first strip in half lengthwise. Mark the strip in a manner similar to that detailed in the Scarface instructions (page 21), with one major exception: The vertical line for this border should be drawn ½" (rather than 1") from the paper crease. Once all marks have been made and diagonal lines drawn, cut along diagonals. Unfold the paper. Fold up the point of each V cut so that it touches the point of the next V.

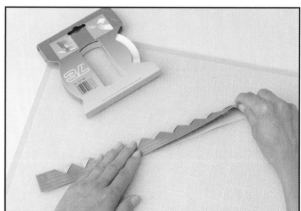

TWO When all V's have been folded, refold the strip along its crease. (Take care to assure that folded V's remain in place). Adhere the folded strip together so that the fold will stay in place. Create a second strip. Mount both strips with notched edges facing each other on torn paper strip to form the border.

Jill Tennyson, Lafayette, Colorado

Miracle

Re-create the look of a quilt without ever picking up a needle. Mat photo on cardstock. Create the scored patterned paper by following the instructions on the right. Cut the scored paper into two pieces (one should be larger than the other). Attach these cut vellum pieces to the page with decorative brads. Place photo over vellum. Add a journaling block and adorn it with fiber. Adhere metal eyelet letters and metal hearts to the page. Mat the entire page on contrasting cardstock.

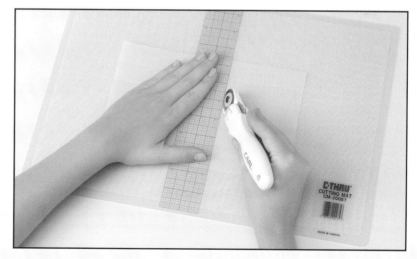

ONE Cut a 6 x 10" vellum rectangle. Using the perforating blade on a rotary trimmer, make 1" vertical passes across the piece of vellum. Turn the vellum 90 degrees and repeat the process, creating a grid. Turn the vellum on the diagonal and mark it in a similar fashion. Turn the vellum once again in the opposite direction and continue making diagonal scores.

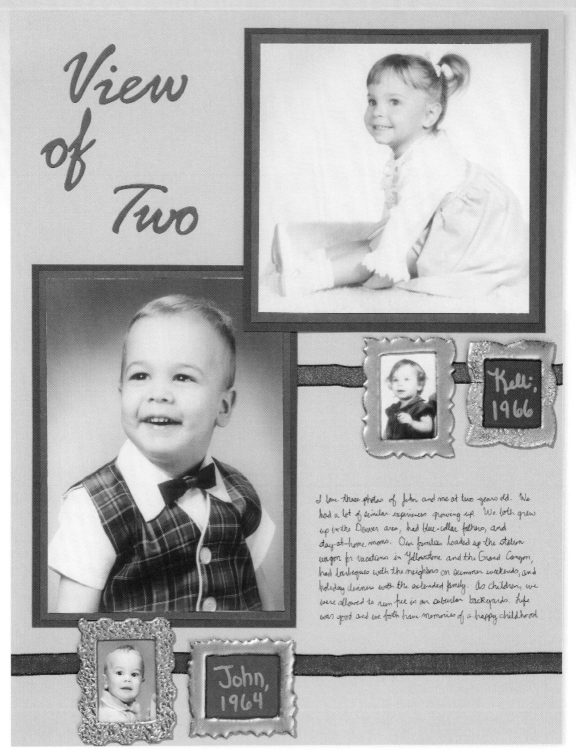

I love these photos of John and me at two years old. We had a lot of similar experiences growing up. We both grew up in the Denver area, had blue-collar fathers, and stay-at-home moms. Our families loaded up the station wagon for vacations in Yellowstone and the Grand Canyon, had barbeques with the neighbors on summer weekends, and holiday dinners with the extended family. As children, we were allowed to run free in our suburban backyards. Life was good and we both have memories of a happy childhood.

Kelli Noto, Centennial, Colorado

View of Two

Create your own custom "metal" frames with decorative scissors (see instructions on adjacent page). Double mat photos and die cut the title. Add ribbon for decoration. Journal to complete the layout.

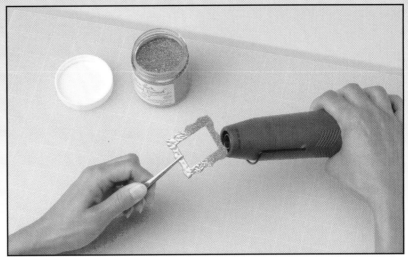

ONE To create the decorative frames seen on the page View of Two (left), cut tagboard rectangles or squares to the desired size. Cover the tagboard pieces with double-sided tacky tape. Cut out the middle of each piece to create a rough frame. Trim the edges of the frame with decorative scissors.

TWO Remove the backing from the tape. Holding the frame with tweezers, dip it into ultra thick embossing enamel (UTEE) until completely covered. Gently shake off the excess enamel. Heat from underneath with a heat gun to melt the embossing powder. For a smoother finish, apply two to four coats of embossing powder, heating between each coat.

Renaissance Festival

The word "Renaissance" conjures up dreamy images of castles and kings, a theme supported by this layout of misty borders and elegant frames created by decorative scissors. Cut a 12" piece of cardstock using decorative scissors. Lay the cut strip near the edge on the background paper. Apply chalk using the decoratively cut strip as a template. Move the strip inward slightly and apply a second color of chalk. Cut mats for pictures. Cut mat edges using decorative scissors. Apply embossing ink to mats and emboss with soft metallic peach embossing powder.

Dawn Mabe, Lakewood, Colorado

The Harris Family

50th Wedding Anniversary
Edwin Andrews Harris
&
Dora Anderton Harris

Robert
Moe
Harris
1840 – 1924

Eloise
Andrews
Harris
1842 –1909

June 1960

Kim Rudd, Idledale, Colorado

The Harris Family

Use both the positive and negative pieces of chains created with decorative scissors to form an elegant border (see instructions below). Adhere the border to the background page, making sure to start and finish the process with a negative piece. Add triangle pieces of cardstock over corners to conceal ends of strips. Double mat photos. Print title and journaling blocks on vellum. Use an oval cutter to trim the edges of two journaling blocks so that they follow the curve of the photos. Attach vellum to the page with gold thread.

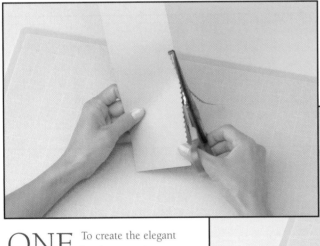

ONE To create the elegant border seen above, use decorative scissors to cut the edge of a 12" piece of cardstock. Set aside this cut piece.

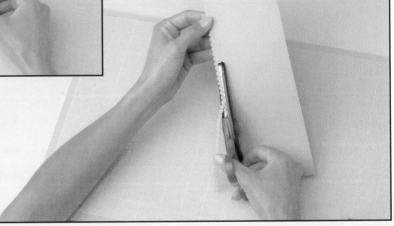

TWO Turn the 12" piece of cardstock over and make a second cut to create a beaded chain effect. Set this piece aside. Use a trimmer to cut a straight ⅛" strip along the edge of the 12" piece of paper. This final border strip should be similar to the first piece you set aside.

Rain

Create themed charms using shrink plastic. Lightly sand shrink plastic. With colored pencils, draw designs on shrink plastic. Make designs three times larger than you wish the final charm to be. Use decorative scissors to cut out the design. Before baking, punch a $\frac{1}{8}$" hole in each charm for hanging. Bake plastic according to the manufacturer's directions. Note: Plastic curls during shrinking process but will usually flatten out when the shrinking process is complete. Place mesh down the right side of the page. Cut irregular shapes out of cardstock and adhere to the mesh. Attach the charms to the cardstock shapes with connected jump rings or pieces of chain. Die cut the title and place it on the torn cardstock. Ink the edges of the title letters. Mat photos on one piece of contrasting cardstock and mount.

Kelli Noto, Centennial, Colorado

Keychain Variations

Use shrink plastic and decorative scissors to create keychains, luggage tags, jewelry and other fun pieces. Use them on scrapbook pages, or keep them for collections.

Kelli Noto, Centennial, Colorado

Valerie Barton, Flowood, Mississippi

Azaleas

Create this fractured mat with decorative scissors and silver thread. Cut the mat out of cardstock. Wrap metallic thread randomly around the mat (see instructions on adjacent page). Adhere the mat to the background and mount the focal photo. Print the vertical title on torn vellum and adhere it to the background. Mount supporting photos. Print journaling block on torn vellum and place it over the supporting photos. Attach with decorative brads.

ONE To create the "shattered" mat seen on the Azaleas page (left), cut the edges of a mat with decorative scissors.

TWO Wrap metallic thread in random patterns around the cut mat using the notches created by the scissor pattern to secure the threads. Adhere the ends of the thread on the backside of the mat.

Dawn Mabe, Lakewood, Colorado

Spirograph

Childhood memories of playing with the Spirograph come sweeping back with just one look at this page. Cut cardstock circles using three decorative scissors that have three different patterns. Wrap funky fibers around the circles, using the notches created by the decorative scissors to secure the fibers. Set an even number of mini-eyelets in a circle on background page. Thread colored wire through eyelets in desired pattern. Mat photos, title and journaling block.

Kelli Noto, Centennial Colorado

Winter Walk

Add a modern twist to good old fashioned paper snowflakes by cutting them with decorative scissors (see instructions on the right and on adjacent page). Embellish snowflakes with glitter and adhere them to the page. Triple mat focal photo and add wrapped fiber. Single mat secondary photos. Mount photos. Die cut a title and journal.

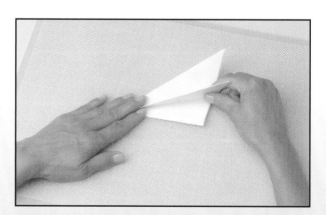

ONE   Cut snowflakes from a 3 x 3" sheet of paper. Fold paper in half diagonally to form a triangle. Refold three more times, creating smaller triangles with each fold.

Bloom Where You're Planted

The illusion of pressed flowers is created with decorative scissors on this colorful page. Make the flower border by cutting different sizes of circles out of colored tissue paper using a variety of decorative scissor patterns. Gather each circle in its center to form a flower shape. Combine multiple circles of the same or varying colors to create more interesting flowers. Secure flowers by wrapping wire around the back of the gathered centers. Cut leaf shapes from mulberry paper and twist wire around their bases to secure. Journaled tags and fibers round off the embellishments.

Jennifer Mason, Longmont, Colorado

TWO Use decorative scissors to cut away small portions of paper along all three sides of the triangle. Make sure that portions of some folds are left intact. Cutting away all edges results in a snowflake that will fall apart.

THREE Unfold paper and flatten. Decorate the snowflake with glitter glue, chalks or watercolors to customize the snowflake and make it truly one of a kind.

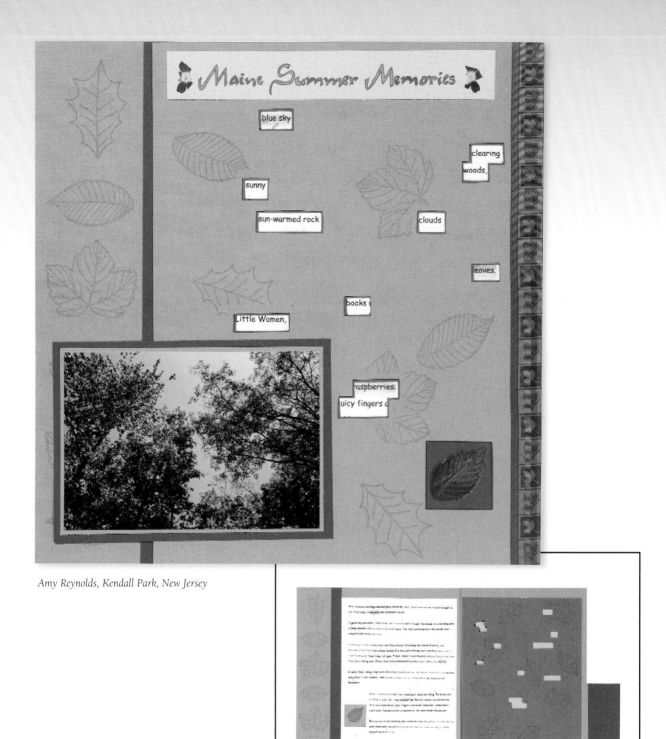

Amy Reynolds, Kendall Park, New Jersey

Maine Summer Memories

Create peek-a-boo windows in a dramatic layout. Stamp watermark leaf images on light green and darker green cardstock. Cut a 3" strip from the left side of the stamped cardstock and set the strip aside. Create windows (see instructions on adjacent page). Double mat photo and mount to the top page overlapping left side edge. Attach the printed journaling block to the bottom page along with the 3" strip which you previously set aside and a ¾" wide strip of purple cardstock. Embellish the page with dried flowers, leaves and a title.

ONE Print journaling on paper. Choose words to be highlighted in "windows." Use a ruler to measure the placement of those words in relation to the edges of the paper. Also note the height and length of the words in order to determine the size required for each window. Transfer your measurements to the previously stamped dark cardstock and draw window rectangles. Cut out windows in dark cardstock with craft knife.

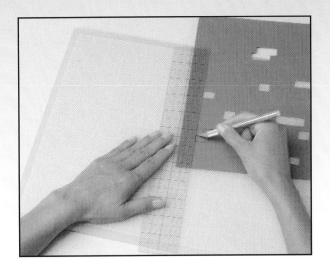

TWO Position dark cardstock on top of stamped light green cardstock. Trace along the inside edges of the windows. Lift dark cardstock and set aside. Use a craft knife to cut windows that are slightly larger than the traced lines on the light cardstock. Punch a 1½" square from the light green cardstock. Mount a dried leaf on the dark green cardstock so the leaf can be viewed through punched square. Cover the leaf with a piece of acetate. Adhere light green stamped cardstock to the front of the darker green page, aligning the windows and creating a matted effect for each window.

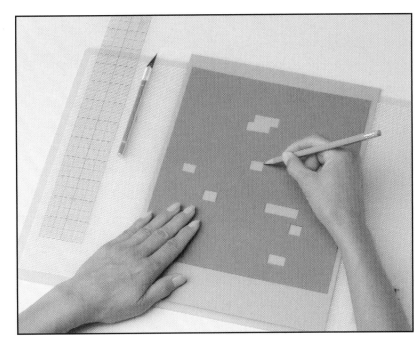

THREE Mount journaled paper along the right edge of a separate sheet of 12 x 12" light green cardstock. Turn journaled page over. Place the page in which you've cut windows face up to the right of the overturned journaled page. To create the binding which will hold these two sections together, place double-sided adhesive tape along the inside edges of both pieces of paper; apply ribbon along edges.

Torrey Miller, Thornton, Colorado

Dance, Play, Smile…Dream

Create a textural mat using a craft knife, fibers and embellishments of your choice (see instructions below). Mat the photo and add metal corners. Adhere metal charms and words to the page. Cover a few charms with plastic watch crystals. Adhere a mesh border across the bottom of the page. Mat a grouping of small photos on torn cardstock. Weave fiber and eyelet letters through slits cut in the bottom of the mat. Use self adhesive foam spacers to mount this photo block to the page.

ONE To create the woven mat on the Dance, Play, Smile…Dream page (above), mark two parallel lines ½" and 1½" from the mat's left edge. Use a craft knife to make random perpendicular slits between these lines. Weave fibers, threaded through a tapestry needle, through the slits. Turn the mat over and adhere it to the background.

Path to the Sea

Weave a decorative border using the same technique featured on the Dance, Play, Smile...Dream page (left). Mat the border on contrasting cardstock. To create the mat, cut cardstock, adhere photo and embellish with fibers. Print the title, mount and decorate with contrasting colors of cardstock strips.

Pat Lingwall, Kennesaw, Georgia

Customize Your Woven and Embellished Border With...

Ribbon and tiny silk flowers

Film negatives and slide frames

Measuring tape and buttons

Hemp and leaves or small pebbles

Paper strips and punches

Wire and beads

Metallic thread and rhinestones

Embroidery floss and charms

Unraveled paper yarn with flat wooden shapes

Grasses and dried flowers

Rickrack and decorative buttons

Lace with string of pearls

Chain and nuts or washers

Leather strips and conchos

Cotton packing twine, brown paper and postage stamps

Satin cording and movie tickets

Curling ribbon and mini bows

Fake fur or braided doll's hair and tiny barrettes

Kelli Noto,
Centennial, Colorado

Custer State Park, South Dakota 8/02

Where the

Buffalo Roam

Where the Buffalo Roam

Cut-out features embellish this Wild West layout (see instructions below). Use the same technique to cut out title words. Create slits for photos in background paper. Mount the entire page on black cardstock with self adhesive foam spacers to lift it off of the background.

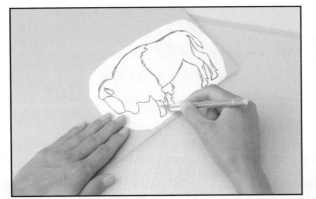

ONE To create the buffalo seen on the page above, draw or copy the desired image on a separate sheet of paper. Use temporary adhesive to stick the drawn image to the front side of cardstock background. Cut on top and bottom of the drawn pattern lines with a craft knife. Leave portions uncut for added visual impact and to secure design.

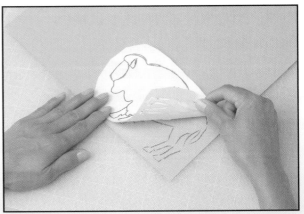

TWO Peel off the pattern and remove residual adhesive with adhesive pickup. Complete page as described above.

Nicole La Cour (Memory Makers), Lochbuie, Colorado.

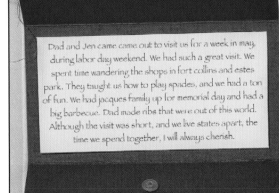

Estes Park

Use a craft knife and cardstock to create powerful photo frames. Mat photo on cardstock, leaving a ½" mat border on all sides. Use a craft knife to cut parallel slices around the mat, creating a rough "fringe." Weave a thin strip of patterned paper through the slices along each side of the mat and secure the ends with glue. Create a hidden journaling block by mounting journaling on a tri-folded piece of cardstock. Use buttons and tinsel to fasten. Embellish with punched cardstock shapes wrapped in tinsel. Chalk tags and place title letter stickers on top. Adhere metal letters. Mat the entire page.

Jodi Amidei, Memory Makers
Photo, Kelli Noto, Centennial, Colorado

Daddy's Girl

Use punches to create a stunning frame (see instructions on adjacent page). Adhere framed photo to background. Print title and journaling on patterned paper and cut it into strips. Stick strips on the background and secure with brads. Wrap fiber between brads. Mount the entire page on solid cardstock.

ONE To create the frame seen on the Daddy's Girl page (left), draw the appropriately sized frame outline on a sheet of paper. Punch your preferred shape from a sheet of cardstock. Randomly place the punched shape within the frame's border, leaving a connection at the side or middle of the frame. Trace around the punched shape. Move the punched shape to a new spot, placing it at an arbitrary angle. Trace. Repeat until the frame is filled. Lightly color in the traced shapes. These will remain uncut.

TWO Adhere the marked frame to a sheet of patterned paper with temporary adhesive. Use a craft knife to cut away the portions of the image which remain uncolored around each punch shape.

THREE

Carefully peel away the frame pattern and remove excess adhesive from the patterned paper with adhesive pickup. Apply a thin strip of tacky tape to the outside and inside edges of the frame. Remove the tape backing and cover with clear microbeads.

SHAPE CUTTERS
PUNCHES
DIE CUTS

Imagine, for a moment, a scrapbooking world without shape cutters. Picture yourself drawing and laboriously cutting intricate shapes by hand. True, it could be done, but few of us would take the time or put forth the effort to agonize over carving complex patterns or designs. So, thank goodness for shape cutters, punches and die cuts! They open up a world of possibilities and save us oodles of time. Most scrapbookers have purchased their fair share of these tools; however, cost prohibits many from owning a true collection and that is reason enough to breathe new life into the ones you do own. This chapter offers some truly unique uses for these tools to produce some fabulous design elements. So dust off those die-cut machines, polish those punches and shine up those shape cutters. It's time to create!

Jill Tennyson, Lafayette, Colorado

How Suite It Is

The Circle Scissor by EK Success is used to create unique corners for this special page. Use the Circle Scissor to cut a number of concentric quarter circles out of cardstock. Mat photos and weave the corner of one mat through the rings created by Circle Scissor cuts. Corners can be made in various sizes and may hold memorabilia as well as photos. Add fiber-embellished tags with letter stickers to create a title and journaling.

It Is a Happy Talent...

Simplicity is beauty, as evidenced by this page, created with the use of a nested-shape template. Print the title and journaling directly onto the background page. On the upper left side and bottom right corner of the page, cut seven concentric half circles using the template and a swivel craft knife. Use the craft knife to cut away every other ring. Bend the inner circle over to secure the photo. Mat the entire page on contrasting cardstock.

Faye Morrow Bell, Charlotte, North Carolina

Sonja Chandler, Brentwood, Tennessee

Austin

Play peek-a-boo on your scrapbook page with hidden journaling windows created by cutting half circles in cardstock with a circle template and a craft knife. Score a straight line at the back of the half circle to aid in opening the window. Adhere a journaling page behind the windows so that words peek through the openings. Make larger windows to accommodate photos. Use a lettering template to cut out a title; add penwork for detail. Mat the photos with patterned paper. Label windows with stamped numbers for easier identification.

Within the image:
- What I love about you...
- that you want to sleep with your sister at night instead of in your own crib
- that you give sweet hugs and kisses
- your genuine excitement about life
- that you try soooo hard to talk
- that you love your big sister
- that you call and call and call my name in the morning until I come and get you
- FEB 2003
- BRINLEY

Brandi Ginn, Lafayette, Colorado

Brinley

Circle and oval cutters were used to create the journaling tags and envelope on this layout. Print journaling on cardstock and cut into varied sizes of circles and ovals. Make a cardstock envelope using an oval cutter. Fold up bottom edge and fold sides in to create the envelope. Emboss the edges of the envelope with copper embossing powder and stamp title. Emboss tags with copper embossing powder, using smaller tags as masks. Embellish tags with eyelets, small punches and fibers. Create a textured frame using modeling paste spread upon cardstock and washed with walnut ink. Finish the frame with brads and metal tag accents. Add torn papers to the background, stitching one into place before securing page elements with adhesive.

Don't Judge Each Day...

This fun and innovative envelope, made with a circle cutter, can be used as an embellishment to hide journaling or to hold a photo or memorabilia. You can even use it as an envelope for handmade cards. Print journaling on vellum. Tear vellum into a strip and wrap it around the envelope. Decorate with stickers, die cuts, tags, fibers or brads!

Denise Johnson for EK Success Ltd.

Create the envelope by cutting a 4 x 4" square of cardstock. Cut four 4" diameter circles. Fold each circle in half to crease. Open each circle. Place a circle crease along the outer edge of the 4 x 4" cardstock square. Adhere. Turn the cardstock square 180 degrees and repeat the process with subsequent circles. Turn the envelope over. Fold the envelope's sides inward and follow with the bottom and top. Decorate the envelope as desired. Create a torn vellum journaling sleeve to hold the envelope closed.

Jodi Amidei, Memory Makers
Photos, Kelli Noto, Centennial, Colorado

Tom and Jodi

Positive and negative space work together to create a big-hearted page. Use a nested template to create the hearts (see instructions on adjacent page). Apply a thin line of glue to the edges of cut hearts and sprinkle with gold micro beads. Adhere photos to page and embellish photos with micro beads. Add vellum journaling strips to the bottom of each photo. Use gold letter stickers to create the title. Mount the entire page on a contrasting background.

ONE Place a nested heart template on patterned background paper. Use a swivel blade to carefully cut all channels. The top and bottom portions of the heart shapes must remain separated by a small portion of uncut paper. Cut along this uncut line when removing unwanted sections of the heart, as follows: Cut away every other section of the upper half of the heart and every other section of the lower portion of the heart. Upper and lower sections being removed should be offset. Repeat the process to create the second heart.

TWO Trim off a small portion of both the top and left sides of the page. Mat the page on a patterned paper background. Embellish the hearts with gold microbeads, as described.

Moonlight Dreams

Romance is in the air on this dreamy page decorated with moon shapes cut from cardstock with a circle cutter. Cut a circle. Remove the circle cutter and reposition it, slightly skewed, on top of the previously cut circle. Re-cut to form a crescent shape. Repeat until all moon shapes are cut. Embellish the crescents with glitter along one edge. Adhere coordinating lace stickers, silk flowers and crescents on the page.

Dawn Mabe, Lakewood, Colorado

May 8, 1992   Gateway Senior Prom

"Set The Night To Music" was the
theme for my prom which took place
at the Palace Inn in Monroeville,
Pennsylvania. I took Mark Paat, a
very good friend of mine, and we
danced, laughed, and had a great time.
The dress I picked out was a Spanish
styled dress that "poofed" out on the
shoulders and on the bottom. (In my
defense, that was the style at the time!)
Mark and I even made the local
newspaper. Ah, high school memories.

*Janetta Wieneke, Memory Makers
Photos, Erlinda Abucejo, Broomfield,
Colorado; Flor Paat, North Huntington,
Pennsylvania*

Prom Memories

Make a quick layout embellishment using a circle scissor as a template. Start
with black cardstock and draw concentric circles (see instructions on adjacent
page). Adhere circles to the page. Add photos and journaling. Build the title out
of two sets of letters die cut from metallic papers. Overlap letters when mounting them to the page in order to create the shadow effect. Complete the layout
with decorative photo corners.

TWO Use a craft knife, scissors or the circle scissor to cut along the rim of the circle you have drawn. Erase the center mark and place a brad in the middle of the circle.

ONE To create the Prom Memories page (left), lightly mark a piece of black cardstock to indicate the center of the circle you will be creating. Place the circle scissor above that mark. Using the circle scissor as a guide, draw concentric circles with silver and red pencils, alternating colors.

So Cozy

Use a circle scissor to create an effect similar to that featured on the Prom Memories page (left). On a white piece of cardstock, lightly mark pencil guidelines which will help you align the scissor. With a watercolor pencil, draw a circle using the circle scissor as a template. Remove the scissor from the page and lightly brush water over watercolor pencil guidelines to bleed the color. Dry. Place the circle scissor back on the paper using the penciled guidelines to realign. Continue drawing concentric circles, one at a time; paint and dry. When the desired circle size has been achieved, cut it out. Erase penciled guidelines. Adhere thin metallic sticker strips randomly to the background page. Adhere cut circles. Double and triple mat photos. Add a vellum sticker title edged with sticker strips.

Pennie Stutzman, Broomfield, Colorado

Diana Swensen for Fiskars

Bodie Island Lighthouse

Make a woven paper border using a shape template and decorative scissors (see instructions below). To create the background, cut a "light beam" out of yellow paper mounted on top of blue background paper. Cover background with printed vellum. Adhere the border to the background. Double mat photo and add matted journaling block.

BODIE ISLAND LIGHTHOUSE

BODIE ISLAND LIGHTHOUSE IS LOCATED HALFWAY BETWEEN THE CURRITUCK BEACH AND CAPE HAT-TERAS LIGHTHOUSE. IT WAS COMPLETED IN 1872 AND THE HEIGHT OF TOWER IS 165 FEET. NC LIGHTHOUSES ARE TRULY BEAUTIFUL AND OUR VISITS TO SEE THEN HAVE BEEN A HIGHLIGHT FOR OUR FAMILY SINCE WE MOVED HERE.

ONE Cut a 1¼ x 11" strip of white cardstock; set aside. Cut another strip of blue cardstock 2 x 11". Use a pencil to lightly mark the center of the backside of the blue strip by creating horizontal and vertical lines which cross in the middle. Place the tip of the diamond shape template on the center mark. Use a pencil to trace only the top half of the diamond. Move the template ½" down the strip and trace the entire diamond. Move template ½" farther down the strip and trace only the bottom half of the diamond. Turn the blue strip upside down and repeat the process for the second half of the strip. Make vertical pencil marks ¼" in from both sides. To make cutting easier, erase all lines that fall beyond these vertical lines toward the outside edges. With a craft knife, cut along pencil marks of diamond shapes.

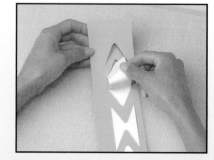

TWO Use the white strip of cut cardstock to weave through the cuts made in the blue strip. Use decorative scissors to cut the right side of the blue strip. Cut another strip of white paper with the same decorative scissors and place it behind the blue strip's edge to shadow. Stamp images on the white strip. Stamp a separate image onto white cardstock and cut it out with the diamond template. Mount this element and adhere to the middle of the border strip.

Sisters Are Forever Friends

Breezy punched pinwheel ornaments adorn this sweet layout. Double mat photo and place it on a patterned paper background. Print the title on vellum and cut it out. Tear a solid-colored cardstock strip and adhere it across the bottom of the page to build the border's base. Attach colored brads to the torn cardstock strip. Create pinwheel ornaments (see instructions below). Adhere pinwheels to the cardstock border. Add a printed journaling strip.

Emily and Kayla Swensen 1999

Sisters are forever friends

Diana Swensen for Fiskars

ONE Punch cardstock using a 1½" square punch. Along one edge of the punched square, align a border punch on the left half and punch (see photo). Rotate the cardstock square 90 degrees and punch again in the same manner. Continue rotating the cardstock square and punching until all sides are punched. Round corners, if desired.

Jordan Kennedy

Make this decorative frame using punches to create a unique stencil (see instructions below). Place a mesh strip along the right side of the background page. Tear strips of coordinating patterned paper and adhere them across the bottom of the layout. Mat photos on cream cardstock and gently ink with dauber. Print journaling and title on transparency film and attach them to the page with colored brads. Mat the entire page and focal photo on contrasting cardstock.

A baby is a small
member of the family
that makes love
stronger, days shorter,
nights longer,
the bankroll smaller,
the home happier, clothes
shabbier,
the past forgotten
and the future worth living
for.

Jordan Kennedy ~ May, 2003

Jodi Amidei, Memory Makers

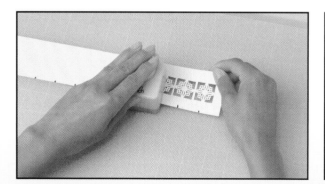

ONE Cut a 2 x 12" strip of light-colored cardstock. To make perfectly spaced punches, boldly mark 1" increments along the strip's edge. Align the left outer edge of the punch casing on a mark and press firmly. Continue punching along the strip, moving the left side of the punch to subsequent marks. When completed, this punched strip will serve as a stencil for inking.

TWO Place the punched stencil on white cardstock and daub ink through the pattern. Rotate the cardstock 90 degrees and repeat the inking process. Continue rotating the cardstock and inking until all four sides are complete. Trim outer edges as needed. Cover the stamped mat with tacky tape and adhere clear micro beads.

What a Clown

Create a cute 3-D doll from tiny circle punched shapes (see directions below). Triple mat photo and adhere it to the background paper. Hand letter or use a template to make the title and journaling blocks and mat. Add the doll embellishment to the page.

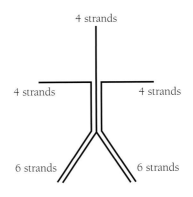

Alison Lindsay, Edinburgh, England

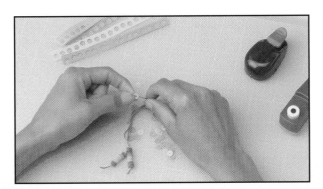

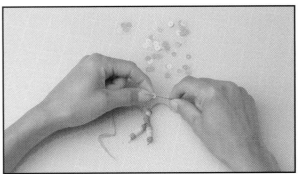

ONE To make paper "sequins" for the clown (above) use a 1/16" hole punch to make several holes along the edge of a piece of cardstock, leaving 1/4" between holes. Take a standard hole punch; center it over each tiny hole and repunch. To create the doll's legs, thread a needle with six-strand embroidery floss. Knot one end. String on sequins. Alternate colors as desired. Set aside, and repeat for the second leg. When the second leg is complete, gather all twelve-strands of floss through the needle and string on sequins to create the doll's body.

TWO When the body is complete, remove the needle and separate the floss into three sections. Each section will now have four strands (see diagram). Rethread the needle with one section of the floss. String on sequins for the arm and finish with a knot. Repeat for the second arm. To form the head, string a few sequins onto the remaining floss section. Add a pearl bead, followed by a few more sequins for the "hat." When complete, knot the floss above the hat, leaving extra floss from which to hang the embellishment on the page. Trim away excess floss.

Chris and Sarah talked all morning about the giant Snowman they were going to build. After lunch I bundled them up and sent them out to build their Snowman. On the way out the door I gave them a little advice, "Start with a ball of snow and build the Snowman from that." Little did I know that ball of snow would be the giant Snowman.

January 1991

Traci Armbrust for Accu-Cut

The Giant Snowman

Use a die cut to create a fun shaker box (see instructions on adjacent page). Mat photos on white cardstock and outline both photos and mat with chalk, using a blender pen to intensify the color. Adhere photos to the patterned paper background. Die cut a snowflake and place it under a vellum journaling block; attach with colored brads. Adorn photo mats with torn strips of coordinating patterned paper, wire and beads. Secure wire to brads. Embellish the layout and shaker box with decorative snowflake buttons. Attach the shaker box to the page and decorate with chalked paper elements and tiny buttons.

ONE   Cut 5 x 5" pieces of foam core and solid color cardstock. Place the foam core and cardstock together on top of the rubber cutting surface of a snowman-shaped die. Run the die through a die-cut machine. Remove the snowman shapes and set aside. Mount on patterned paper the piece of foam core from which the snowman has been cut. Seal carefully along all edges. Adhere a sheet of acetate (slightly smaller than 5 x 5") to the backside of the piece of cardstock from which the snowman has been cut. Cut snowman arms, hat and scarf from cardstock using the die-cut machine. Insert the arms in the cardstock snowman shape and adhere to acetate. Chalk the hat and scarf, and adhere to the snowman.

TWO   Fill the foam core snowman shape with beads and shaved ice. Adhere the blue cardstock snowman cover, acetate side down, to the foam core snowman. Make certain all edges are sealed so the shaker box contents don't leak out.

Sun Kissed

Shake up your page with a sunny shaker box. Punch three large squares out of a decorative border strip. Save punched squares to use as embellishments. Mount the border strip on torn cardstock. Create the shaker box by adhering a piece of acetate behind the punched windows. Lay strips of foam tape around the outer edges of the punched window piece, taking care to avoid gaps (it is unnecessary to lay foam around each individual window). Sprinkle small punches, beads, and other trinkets into windows. Peel the backing away from foam tape and adhere to torn cardstock strip. Mat photo and page. Add a sticker title.

Denise Johnson for EK Success Ltd.

Heidi Schueller,
Waukesha, Wisconsin

Watcing a little boy watching frogs is an unforgettable experience! Exploring one afternoon while camping at Upper Gresham Lake, we came across some children playing with two huge bullfrogs. After they let them go, Evan, Karen and I grabbed a camera and took some pictures. Evan was amazed and entranced watching it hop around.

Camp Hop

Make movable embellishments that "spring" to life using your die-cut machine (see instructions on this and adjacent page). Cut "camp" title letters out of cardstock, mat and mount on background. Cut out "hop" from colored vellum, embossing the letter edges. Mat and mount on background. Mat photos using fibers on the edge of the focal picture. Suspend fibers and beads from brads. Print the journaling on vellum and emboss the edges.

Make the frogs "hop" by gently pulling back and forth on the end of the base strip.

ONE Die cut five frogs from two shades of cardstock (three light/two dark). Cut apart the legs of the darker frogs. Glue dark sets of legs on two of the lighter colored bodies. On the remaining light colored frog, adhere a dark body. Glue a small piece of colored cardstock behind each frog's eyes to add stability when securing the brads.

These Boots Are Made For Walking

Make a border that literally dances (see instructions for Camp Hop below and on adjacent page). Die cut small cardstock dolls. Add embellishments such as hair and shiny black embossed cardstock boots. Make a doll border strip. Create shiny cardstock photo mats with black embossing powder. Add decorative metal brads and flowers. Mat a vellum journaling block on cardstock. Add strips of foil as accents. Attach flower accents with bits of chain.

Heidi Schueller, Waukesha, Wisconsin

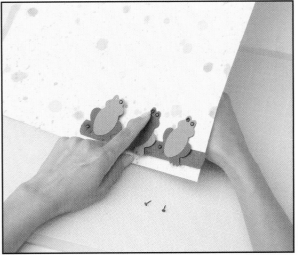

TWO Punch a ¹⁄₁₆" hole in the right foot of each frog. Cut two ¼ x 8" strips of brown cardstock, and adhere them to each other to create the "log" pull strip on which frogs are attached. Align the frogs evenly along the log, leaving 1" on the right end. Make pencil marks through the holes in the frogs' feet onto the log. Punch ¹⁄₁₆" holes into the log on the marks. Attach the frogs' right feet to the log with brads.

THREE Punch ¹⁄₁₆" holes for the frogs' eyes. Line up the frogs on background paper and mark through each right eye-hole to the background paper underneath. Punch holes in the background paper. Use a brad to fasten each frog's right eye to the background paper. Place a brad in the left eye openings for decoration. Add penwork details to the log. Add a decorative eyelet or brad to the end of the handle.

Jodi Amidei, Memory Makers
Photos, Chrissie Tepe, Lancaster,
California

Children Are God's Way…

You'll love the effect you'll get by softly tearing heart edges with a die (see instructions on adjacent page). With watermark ink, randomly stamp a design onto solid cardstock background. Tear patterned paper and cardstock to create the border; adhere it to the background and gently roll the torn edges. Create the frame by adhering printed and solid paper together. Mark guidelines to indicate the size you wish the frame's opening to be. Note: Make the opening slightly smaller than you envision the finished frame. Cut a small hole in the center of the frame and begin to gently tear away paper until you reach the guideline. Gently roll back the remaining torn edge. Tear the outside edges of the solid paper to desired size. Place photo under the frame opening and mat the entire frame on patterned paper with foam tape. Print journaling on patterned paper and tear to size. Embellish journaling block and frame with wire and beads. Mount frame and journaling to stamped background.

 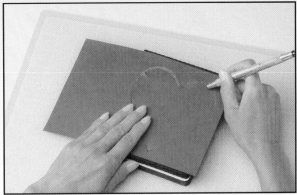

ONE Place cardstock on the rubber side of a die and rub finger gently over the design until a faint outline of the pattern emerges.

TWO While holding cardstock in place on the die, run an impressing tool along the outline until the paper tears. Note: Cutting blades are hidden within the rubber surface so you may need to exert a fair amount of pressure to expose the blades. Do not use your fingers! Adorn the top hearts with clear embossed image and beaded wire.

Flowers

Torrey Miller, Thornton, Colorado

Combine two different die cuts to create these funky flower accents and border. Cut four to five 4 x 4" pieces of contrasting cardstock. Run each piece through a die-cut machine, using a weaving die (Dayco). Set aside one of these pieces. Tear cut strips free from the remaining die cuts. Use these strips to weave alternating colors through the intact die cut. When complete, run the woven piece through an adhesive application machine. Mount the adhered woven piece on a solid piece of cardstock. Die cut flower shapes from the assembled piece. Glue loose ends of weaving to its cardstock backing. Punch holes in flowers and coil wire accent through hole. Use leftover strips of weaving assemblies for page embellishments. Mat photos and the entire page. Add metal title letters.

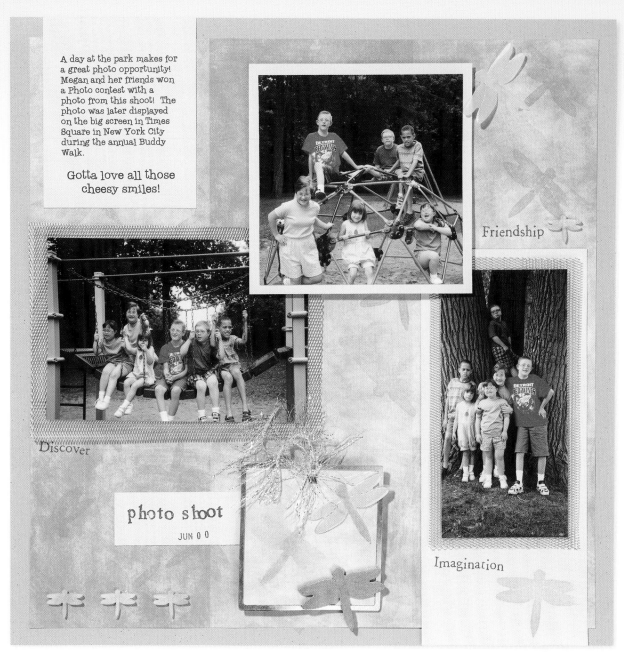

A day at the park makes for a great photo opportunity! Megan and her friends won a Photo contest with a photo from this shoot! The photo was later displayed on the big screen in Times Square in New York City during the annual Buddy Walk.

Gotta love all those cheesy smiles!

Friendship

Discover

photo shoot

JUN 0 0

Imagination

Jennifer Mason, Longmont, Colorado
Photos by: Lucy Talbot, Sterling Heights, Michigan

Photo Shoot

Create shimmery charms and glistening background shapes using a die-cut machine (see instructions on adjacent page). Mat one photo on metal mesh and another on cardstock. Mat the third photo on both mesh and cardstock. Print journaling and adhere to the page. Arrange and adhere photos to the page. Add charms. Create the vellum metal-rimmed tag by stamping a design (in same fashion as the background paper), and adding die-cut dragon-flies and fiber. Stamp words around the page. Mat the entire page on coordinating cardstock.

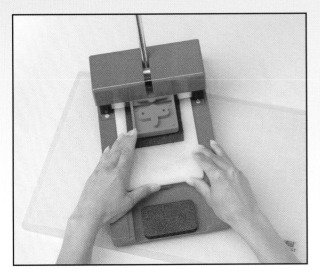 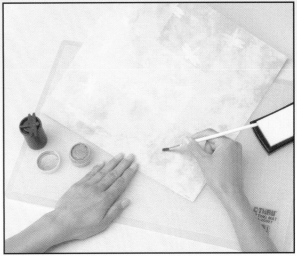

ONE — Using a die-cut machine, cut a dragonfly shape out of craft foam.

TWO — Adhere the die-cut-dragonfly to anything that can be used as a handle for stamping (we used the bottom of an empty film canister). Stamp images onto patterned paper background with watermark ink. With a small brush, dust images with iridescent pigment powder. Gently wipe away excess with a tissue.

Coming Home to Tennessee

Die cut cork for a unique title, aluminum foil for tree accents and hearts and burlap for leaf embellishments. Tear a background of rust-colored patterned paper. Dab dark brown stamping ink along the torn edges. Mat on green patterned paper. Mat photos with tan patterned paper. Create the title using chalked polymer letter tiles adorned with hemp and letter stickers. Cut the word "home" from thin cork and adhere to corrugated paper. Finish the title using eyelet letters and printed mulberry paper mounted on a fiber-embellished tag. Punch leaf shapes from burlap. Use the negative pieces as page embellishments. Complete the layout with die-cut-foil hearts and die-cut trees made of copper sheeting. Mount a vellum journaling block over the trees.

Holle Wiktorek, Clarksville, Tennessee

Our Fall Wedding

Create a stained-glass border using a die-cut machine (Sizzix) and scissors (see instructions on this and adjacent page). Mat and mount photo. Add a journaled block. Create the title by cutting windows in the background paper. Print title on colored vellum and place sections behind each window.

Jan Perilli, Summit Hill, Pennsylvania
Photo, Joe McElnaugh, Jim Thorpe Wedding
Photography Co.

ONE Cut four 3 x 3" squares of different colored cardstock, making certain they are all exactly the same size. Stack the squares on top of each other and cut them all together using a die-cut machine and leaf die. This will ensure they are all identical.

Michigan Lakes

Only half a die cut is needed to create this interesting effect. Mask off half the die with a piece of cutting plastic and run a sheet of two-tone grey cardstock background paper through the die cut machine. (A #3 Spiral die from Accu-Cut was used for this page.) The plastic prevents half of the die from being cut. Score the spiral die cut where the cut ends.

Fold the cut parts up, and adhere them to the background. Place black cardstock behind the cut-out portion. Cut ½" wide strips of patterned cardstock and adhere to the top and left sides of the page. Double mat photos and journaling blocks on grey and black cardstock. Print journaling on vellum and adhere. Add a ½" wide strip of patterned cardstock under the die cut feature. Finish the strip embellishment with silver brads.

Martha Moseman for Accu-Cut

TWO Select two colors of cardstock for the leaves, and two different colors for the borders. Hold identically cut pieces together and cut into pieces as shown. Loosely arrange the pieces on cardstock, alternating colors.

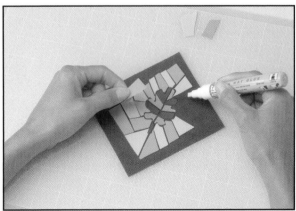

THREE Glue pieces to black cardstock in appropriate position. Make certain to leave a small gap between each piece to create the look of stained glass. Repeat the process to create additional panels.

Easter 2002

We spent Easter Sunday at my mom's house in Newport Beach. The girls were looking super cute in there matching dresses that Shaya picked out. The Easter bunny was exceptionally good to Jessie and Shaya with all the wonderful goodies they got in their Easter baskets, complete with a pair of bunny ears. My mom had an Easter egg hunt in the backyard for everyone including the adults. It brought back lots of great memories of my childhood, which made it special to share with my own children. It was a beautiful sunny day and a great Easter.

HOPPY EASTER

Cara Mariano for Ellison

Hoppy Easter

Make bunnies that march across your page. Accordion-fold paper and use a die-cut machine to create a "paper doll" strip of bunnies (see instructions on adjacent page). To create the background, cut patterned paper on the diagonal and adhere it to a solid cardstock background. Print journaling on patterned paper and adhere it to the background with self-adhesive foam spacers. Mat photos and adhere to the background. Embellish with an extra die-cut bunny.

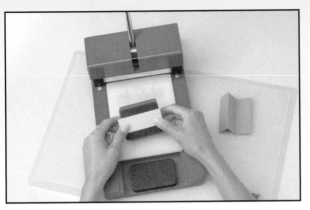

ONE Create the Hoppy Easter page by cutting six 3½ x 3½" squares of colored cardstock (three light/three dark) and folding each into thirds accordion-style. To make bunny chains, make certain the die's cutting surface is slightly wider than the folded paper. Place one piece of accordion-folded paper on the die so the blade is visible on both sides of the bunny. Run the paper through the die-cut machine. This will create a chain of three bunnies. Repeat for remaining five pieces of accordion-folded paper.

TWO Cut apart various portions of the dark bunnies and glue pieces, as desired, to light bunnies. Adhere a small piece of pink cardstock behind the opening in the bunnies' ears and noses. Place black cardstock behind the bunnies' eyes. Add penwork detail and mount the bunnies on the background. Add letter stickers for the title.

Brenee Williams for Provo Craft

Pumpkin Princess

Create this pumpkin chain by folding dark maroon cardstock, accordion-style, into thirds. While folded, use a template to cut a pumpkin shape, leaving 1" along the folded bottom left edge uncut. Print journaling on coordinating orange patterned paper. Use a template to cut journaling blocks into pumpkin shapes slightly smaller than the maroon accordion. Decorate the front of the pumpkin journaling book with patterned paper. Cut stars and place on the background. Attach gold brads to journaling book and star; connect with gold thread. Double mat photo on patterned paper; add tulle corners. Cut a tulle pocket approximately one-third the size of the page and stitch onto the bottom of the layout and around the background with gold thread. Slide the pumpkin journaling book into the tulle pocket.

Never does nature say one thing and wisdom another.
Juvenal

If one way be better than another, that you may be sure is nature's way.
Aristotle

I go to nature to be soothed and healed and to have my senses put in order.
John Burroughs

Let us permit nature to have her way. She understands her business better than we do.
Michel de Montaigne

Man's heart away from nature becomes hard.
Standing Bear

Nature is the art of God.
Thomas Browne

Look deep into nature, and then you will understand everything better.
Albert Einstein

Everything has beauty, but not everyone sees it.
Confucius

I've always regarded nature as the clothing of God.
Alan Hovhaness

Stencils, Templates, Decorative Rulers

Most of us have a penchant for perfection when it comes to making letters for titles. We want exquisite curves, impeccable lines and flawless angles...all without those tell tale pencil lines. This can be effortlessly achieved with the use of templates and stencils. But there is so much more you can do with a stencil, template or decorative ruler than use them as simple lettering guides. It's time to look at your stencils, templates and decorative rulers in a whole new way and to explore their possibilities. Learn how to use these 2-dimensional tools to create intriguing 3-dimensional embellishments and accents for your scrapbook layouts. Keep scrapbooking exciting and fresh by trying new things and your pages will evolve and grow right along with your self-confidence.

Jodi Amidei, Memory Makers
Photos, Torrey Miller, Thornton,
Colorado

Garden Party

Use a brass stencil and polymer clay to create these decorative floral embellishments (see instructions on adjacent page). Double mat photos and place them on the background. Mat a colored torn cardstock strip on a piece of black cardstock for the border; wrap it with fibers and attach on back side. Add polymer tiles. For the title, tear a piece of cardstock and adhere it diagonally across the upper left page corner. Add fiber and adhere the title tile.

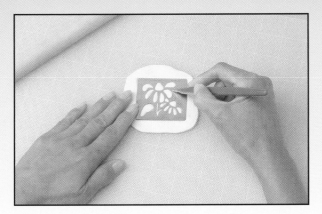

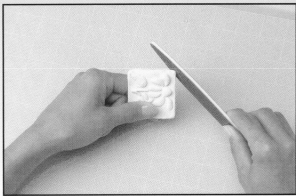

ONE Roll out polymer clay to ⅛" thickness. Use a stylus to press a brass stencil into the clay to make an image. Gently lift the stencil from the clay. Use a craft knife to trim away excess clay. Carefully transfer the "tile" to a glass baking pan and bake according to manufacturer's directions.

TWO When cooled, use an emery board or fine sandpaper to gently sand the edges of the clay tile until smooth and rounded.

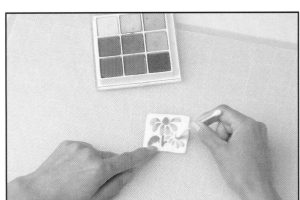

THREE Apply chalk lightly to colorize the image. Add more chalk until the desired effect is achieved. When satisfied with colorized effect, spray with acrylic sealant to fix the color.

Torrey Miller, Thornton, Colorado

Celebrate

Create a unique title with black polymer clay and a word template (see instructions for Garden Party page above). Cut clay to desired shape and bake as directed. Using a metallic leafing pen, color in the raised negative spaces of the word. Mat the clay tile on silver paper with glue dots. For the background, mount patterned paper over silver paper. Place mesh over patterned paper, securing it with decorative brads. Mount the clay title to mesh with glue dots. Attach circular paper clips on torn black cardstock and add metallic fibers.

Valerie Barton, Flowood, Mississippi

Winter White

Create frosty embellishments for a winter page (see instructions on adjacent page). Tear the edges of patterned paper to create a background. Print journaling on the left side of a strip of vellum and attach the strip to the page with eyelets. Mat photos. Place focal photo over the portion of the vellum which does not display journaling. Add a strip of journaled vellum diagonally across the bottom corners of the photo. Make a title with a metal-rimmed vellum tag, letter stickers, letter beads and a ribbon. Add organza ribbon and fiber across the bottom of the page. Embellish with frosty ornaments and mat the entire page.

Lessons Learned From a Lime Green Cast

Use texture paste and stencils to create a well-"cast" title (see instructions for Winter White below). Tear out letters. Add a torn patterned paper strip at the bottom of the layout. Print the remainder of the title and the journaling block on vellum and adhere to the page with decorative brads. Cover a portion of the layout with gauze fabric. Mat the focal photo and embellish its corner with a knotted piece of gauze. Add the smaller photo and a stamped, patterned vellum metal-rimmed tag.

Valerie Barton, Flowood, Mississippi

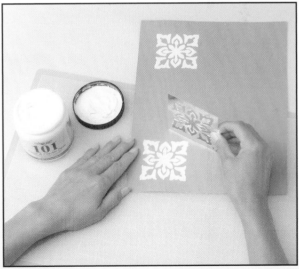

ONE Place a brass stencil on cardstock. While holding down the stencil, use a finger to apply texturizing paste to fill in all areas of the stencil pattern.

TWO Carefully lift off the stencil. The paste will crackle as it dries. Wash paste off your hands and the stencil immediately. Allow the paste to dry completely before tearing edges and adhering it to the layout.

Surely a star danced in heaven on the day you were born.

Faye Morrow Bell,
Charlotte, North Carolina

Surely a Star Danced

Use square and rectangular templates with paint to create a beautiful background. Print journaling on background paper. Lightly pencil outlines of square and rectangular template shapes. Thin acrylic paint with water. Place a template over penciled guide marks and use a sponge to apply paint through the template. Let the paint dry before sponging on a second color. Add photo and Chinese coins to page.

Ya Ya Sisterhood

Use texturizing paste applied through a lettering template to create a title that says it all. While the paste is still wet, sprinkle on colored embossing powder and allow it to dry. Cut out letters and set them aside. (Use a brass stencil for a slightly different look.) With a craft knife, cut out portions of the design running through the background paper. Double mat photo and slip it underneath these cut-free portions. Mount individual title letters on torn blue cardstock. Create flower embellishments by cutting unraveled paper yarn into leaf shapes and rolling it to form flower centers. Make hat embellishments by stamping image, embossing and adding decorative flower. Print journaling onto vellum and attach it to the cardstock mat with eyelets.

Cousins

Combine a rectangle template with rubber stamping to embellish a page that is simply elegant. Print title sideways on the left side of background. Position the template on the background paper and draw the rectangular outline with a fine-tip marker. Holding the template firmly in place, stamp through the opening to create an image that has a perfectly squared border. Print journaling on colored cardstock, and embellish with a template/stamped image. Add photo and fibers.

Sun Goddess

Make your own rubber stamp using a brass stencil and moldable foam (see instructions below). To texturize the top layer of background paper, wet and crumple cardstock. Smooth and iron it dry. Tear a second sheet of cardstock along the right side and curl its edges back. Stitch the texturized background to a second sheet of cardstock at arbitrary points. Add chalk to the cardstock edges and along stitched lines. Mat stitched background pieces to a third layer of cardstock background. Place natural fiber "ribbon" down the left side of the page and attach on the back side. Frame photo using a similar technique as described in Children Are God's Way… (page 58). Print journaling and title on cardstock and cut it into tag shapes. Embellish with fiber and charms. Add chalk to "age" frame, border, title and journal. Attach stamped paper tiles.

Torrey Miller, Thornton, Colorado

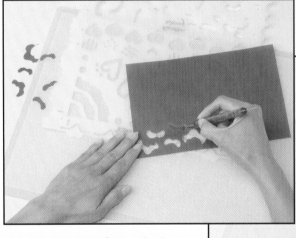

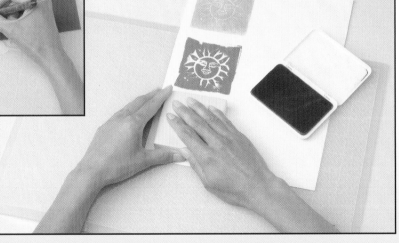

ONE Heat foam with a heat gun and immediately press a brass stencil into the hot foam. You may need to press a finger along the finer details to impress the image. Hold the stencil in place for a few seconds to set the image. Remove the stencil. You now have a reusable rubber stamp.

TWO Ink the impressed foam and stamp onto cardstock. Tear out the stamped designs and chalk the edges for detail. Adhere to the layout.

Love Letter

Create beautiful backgrounds with lettering templates. On an 8½ x 11" piece of white cardstock, rub chalk through the template's larger letter openings. Use a fine-tip marker to outline each letter, including any finely detailed parts that might not have been well-chalked. Mount the lettered background to 12 x 12" cardstock. Cut out a title using another lettering template, and apply it to the left side of the page. Add penwork details, hang a metal-rimmed tag and add a metal charm to the title. To create the photo mat, make a cardstock card which opens on one side and mount it to the background. Inside the card put printed journaling and another matted photo; decorate with a sticker. Place mounted focal photo on the outside of the card.

Mary Anne Walters, Monk Sherborne, Tadley, England

*Mary Anne Walters,
Monk Sherborne,
Tadley, England*

Reading Is Pure Dead Brilliant

Produce unique borders and mats with a lettering template. Cut cardstock mats with ½" borders. Use a lettering template and silver gel pen to decorate the mats. Create the border by drawing vertical lines 2" apart down the outer edges of the layout. Decorate with a lettering template and pen as with the mats. Scan the child's book cover and print the title onto photo paper. While the ink is still wet, sprinkle on embossing powder and heat the embossed title. Cut out the letters with a craft knife and mount them on the background. Embellish with metal letters and brads. Journal on vellum and adhere to cardstock mats.

United in Love

Tear intricate paper-pieced shapes easily and accurately using nothing but a shape template and a stylus (see instructions on adjacent page). Cut large oval windows out of background cardstock. Place photos behind the windows to create frames. Make hand-lettered title banners by tearing strips of vellum and pleating the ends. Add journaling and rose embellishments.

Roxane Kryvenchuk, Edmonton, Alberta, Canada

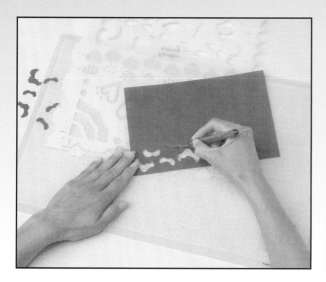

ONE To create the flowers on the United in Love page (left) firmly hold a piece of vellum on top of a template. Using a stylus, outline the template shape until the vellum piece breaks free. Repeat for all desired shape pieces.

TWO Assemble the floral embellishments and adhere the torn vellum pieces directly to the background to form roses. Construct flowers beginning with outer pieces and working inward.

Lazy Days of Summer

Tear perfect letters and shapes out of vellum using a template. Run vellum through an adhesive application machine and peel off the top plastic covering. To make bubble shapes, roughly cut the prepared vellum slightly larger than the bubble shape. Place wax paper on a work surface and lay the template on top. Peel the backing off of the vellum and place the adhered vellum on the template, completely covering the template opening. Using a stylus, trace around the template shape several times until the vellum is cut through and falls onto the wax paper underneath. Remove the vellum shape from the wax paper and adhere it to the page. Create letters the same way using a lettering template. Cut photos with a circle cutter. Mount photos and the title on bubbles. Journal.

Roxane Kryvenchuk, Edmonton, Alberta, Canada

Linda Strauss, Provo, Utah

Help I'm Being Eaten

The scales on the snake's back are made by mirror imaging the boy's name (Mario) with letters cut from a template (see instructions below and on adjacent page). Make the background by crumpling cardstock, flattening it and then securing it to the mat with eyelets. Create a title by hand-lettering on random shapes of torn cardstock and add details with a black pen. Mat photo on torn cardstock. Embellish with gold jewelry findings. Include a real snake skin, enclosed in a memorabilia pocket.

ONE Sketch a snake shape on cardstock and free-hand tear along pattern lines. Attach a cut or torn tongue and tail pieces to the body with glue.

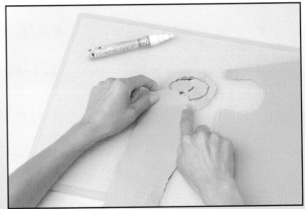

Summertime and the Living Is Easy

The letters that make up your page title can also be part of the page embellishment. Use a computer to write the title. Print the word on plain copy paper in the size desired. Adhere the title to patterned paper with temporary adhesive. Using a craft knife, cut out the individual letters. Peel off the copy paper and remove excess adhesive. Adhere the letters to patterned background in a circular pattern of sun rays. Embellish the page with unraveled paper yarn, eyelets and die cuts. Make journaling tags out of the same patterned paper as used for the title.

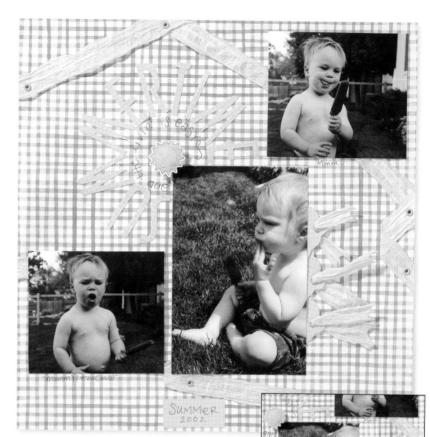

Emily Marjamaa, Fort Collins, Colorado

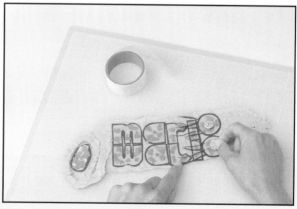

TWO From cardstock, die cut two of each letter needed to spell out the boy's name. One set of letters should be reversed. Mat letters on black cardstock, and decorate the letters with torn pieces of contrasting-colored cardstock. Place the letters mirroring each other onto the snake.

THREE Add torn bits of paper and metallic embellishments to complete the snake.

Brenee Williams for Provo Craft

Grandma Karen's
First Grade Class

Make 3-D metal embellishments using a shape template. Place a medium-weight metal sheet over a template. Using a stylus, trace and "color in" the shape to create a gentle concave-shaped image. Cut out the shape and turn it over. Adhere it to cardstock circles with self-adhesive foam spacers. Cut several circles out of patterned paper for the journaling book. Print journaling onto vellum. Cut the vellum in circles that are slightly smaller than those on the primary page. Adhere them to the pages of the journaling book. Double mat photo and mat the entire page. Use eyelets to secure the fiber holding the embellishments.

JD

Create your own metal letter hanging tags easily. Place a metal sheet over a letter template and place on a neoprene-style mouse pad. Trace around the letter with a stylus. Add your own decorative designs such as swirls, polka dots, stripes, checkerboards, or flowers. Cut out the letter and mat it on cardstock. Hang the letter with wire, eyelets, brads or fibers. Use a precut cardstock background, or make your own by dry embossing the cardstock and cutting out windows with a craft knife. Journal.

Lori Pieper for C-Thru Ruler

Paula Hallinan for Heritage Handcrafts

Nativity Card

Create an ornate nativity card with metal embossing (see instructions). Trim edges with decorative scissors and adhere to cardstock. Mat cardstock with silver paper.

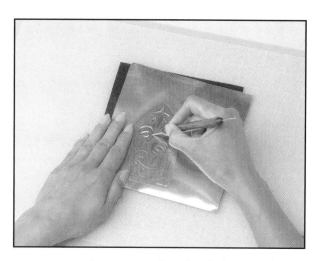

ONE To create an embossed card, place a metal sheet on a neoprene-style mousepad. Cover with a brass stencil and trace the image into metal using a stylus. When complete, remove the stencil and turn the metal sheet over.

This picture of Elizabeth and Zachary is one of Mom's all time favorite shots. It was taken in August of 1999 at the Au Sable Valley Railroad in Fairview. Zach was 10 and Elizabeth was 2. There are so many reasons why this photograph is special to Mom. She loves all of Zach's freckles. She loves all the whispy curls in Elizabeth's hair. She loves Zach's sweet smile. And, she loves Elizabeth's hands with one holding onto Zach and the other with her thumb in her mouth. Mom never gets tired of looking at this picture and every time she does, it pulls at her heart strings.

Beth Wakulsky for Provo Craft

Heart Strings

Specialty papers such as mulberry or thin handmade papers don't stand up well when cut with a craft knife. Make the job easier by applying temporary adhesive to the paper's backside and sticking the fragile paper to a sheet of wax paper. The wax paper backing allows easier cutting with less wear and tear on the paper. When finished cutting out letters and shapes, peel off wax paper backing and adhere cut elements directly to page. Embellish the layout with fabric mesh, buttons and fibers. Secure a vellum journaling block with colored brads.

Sorting Hearts

Make a border using a shape template. Use a pencil to outline the template shape on one side of a piece of white-core cardstock. Move the template over so that the second shape slightly overlaps the first and trace the shape once more. Continue moving the template and tracing until the border is the desired length. Use scissors or a craft knife to cut out the border. Erase pencil marks. To "distress" the border, use fine grit sandpaper to lightly sand the border's edges. Create additional embellishments by chalking through a template onto a piece of cardstock; cut to size. Or trace template shapes, cut out the design, and place mesh or fabric behind the opening left behind. Create a stitched title with embroidery floss and chalk. Adhere mesh and torn strips of patterned paper to a cardstock background. Finish the layout by stamping with a small letter and date stamp.

Marilyn Healey for Provo Craft

Marilyn Healey for Provo Craft

Wind Cave

Use whimsical patterned paper and a lettering stencil to create a unique title. Trace title letters onto white cardstock. Randomly stamp letters over the traced title letters using brown ink. Chalk the letter edges and lightly dab red ink across the letter. Cut out the letter and dab the edges in black ink or hand color the edges with a felt pen. Mount title letters on vellum and weave through them with handcut chalked "wind" swirls. Make background paper by placing large sections of torn patterned paper on a brown cardstock background. Embellish the layout with bits of torn cardstock fiber and chalking. Use both letter stickers and hand lettering to create the remainder of the title and journaling.

Diana Swensen for Fiskars

Fall

Create a woven border using the decorative edge of a shape template (as seen below). Double mat photos and decorate mats with tiny punched leaves. Watermark stamp leaf images onto the background. Mount photos on the background. Cut out letters for titles using a shape-cutting system. Print journaling words on cardstock and cut them into small rectangles. Mat the title and journaling words and adhere them to the background.

ONE Use a Fiskars shapecutter and Celebration template to cut borders along the paper's edge. Punch every other "scallop" with a small leaf punch. On the side strip, punch opposite "scallops" with a different leaf punch. Intertwine the borders so that punched scallops are showing.

Sonja Chandler, Brentwood, Tennessee

Never Lose Your Joy

Create a positive/negative effect across your layout with a wavy ruler (see instructions below). Once wavy pieces have been cut, adhere them to a white cardstock background. Print a title and journaling blocks on vellum and cut using the same wavy ruler used to create the decorative page elements. Mat photos and slide them under the edges of the wavy accents.

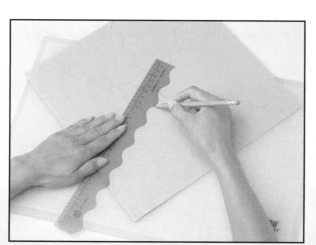

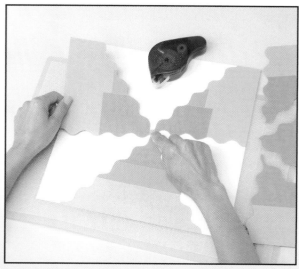

ONE In the center of a 12 x 12" piece of grey cardstock, adhere a 6 x 8" piece of aqua cardstock. Slightly overlapping the aqua, adhere a 5 x 7" piece of blue cardstock to create a layered effect (not shown). Turn the assembly over, and mark the center of the back side of the grey cardstock. Use a decorative ruler to draw "sunburst" rays from the center mark to the edges of the paper. Cut on the lines.

TWO Arrange and adhere the pieces on two separate sheets of white 12 x 12" cardstock to create a two-page layout in a chosen design.

Jill Tennyson,
Lafayette, Colorado
Photos, Torrey Miller, Thornton,
Colorado

Colorado

Create a pattern for a stitched border using a decorative ruler (see instructions below). For the beaded section of the border, lay tacky tape on a separate strip of cardstock and trace the ruler's edge along both long edges of the strip. Cut out the design. Remove the protective backing and adhere gold micro beads along the strip. Adhere the beaded strip onto the background page. Stitch remaining sections of the border. Mat photos and adhere to the background. Stamp a title on vellum and apply journaling sticker. Secure vellum elements to the background with decorative studs. Mat the entire page on colored cardstock.

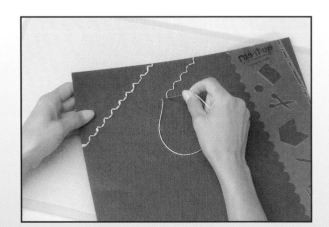

ONE Lay a decorative ruler on cardstock background to use as a pattern. Following the ruler design, pierce holes along the edge of the ruler. Stitch with silk ribbon or embroidery floss.

Janetta Wieneke, Memory Makers

First Time Grandma

Use the edge of a decorative ruler as a template for gluing down a fiber border. Transfer the ruler pattern to cardstock using one of the following methods: Trace the pattern on the backside of paper. Turn the paper over and place it on a light box, (or) use a vanishing pen on light colored cardstock to trace the ruler directly onto the background, (or) lightly outline the ruler pattern on dark cardstock. Adhere fiber along the ruled line. Create background paper by mounting a 9½ x 9½" piece of patterned paper in the center of solid-colored cardstock. Attach the thin ribbon border to the edges of the cardstock background with eyelets. Mount photos with photo corners. Print a title and journaling on vellum mounted on contrasting vellum. String letter beads on embroidery floss and attach them to photos. Add punched shapes decorated with rhinestones.

Friends

Lettering and shape templates act as guides for easily stitched page embellishments. Place a lettering shape template on background paper and pierce holes approximately ⅜" apart. Stitch through the holes with embroidery floss. Use a different template to add the decorative flower, working in the same manner as previously described. Mat photo and page and add a journaling block.

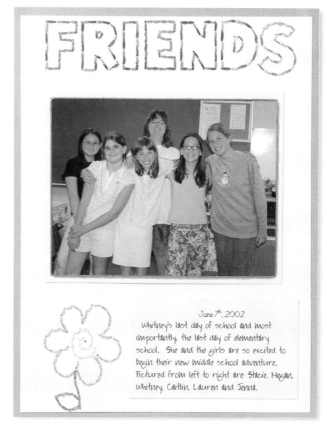

Tracey Mason, Gahanna, Ohio

Roxane Kryvenchuk, Edmonton, Alberta, Canada

Four Wheelin'

A decorative template can help create woven borders and mats (see instructions on adjacent page for border). Cut an oval window from black cardstock and frame the photo. Mat the framed photo on red cardstock and then again on another piece of black cardstock measuring ¼" larger than the red mat. Using a square design decorative template, cut slits in the mat along the sides of the template's "teeth." Work from the center of each side and move toward the corners. Cut a rectangular hole in a separate sheet of red background paper. Make the hole ⅛" larger than the red photo mat. Place matted photo over the cut hole. Weave the "teeth" of the template-cut black mat over and under the edge of the rectangular hole to create a striped effect. Cut off the corner "teeth." To create the title, lightly pencil a diagonal baseline. Sketch blocky letters along the line and cut slits through the background paper along the vertical lines. Do NOT cut the horizontal top and bottom lines. Weave ¼" strips of contrasting cardstock through the slits. For letters with diagonal lines, add a small diagonal strip of cardstock to fill in necessary space. Adhere strips to backside of layout and erase all pencil lines. Make additional slits in the background for journaling. Write journaling on ½" wide strips and weave through slits to anchor. Finish the title with letters cut from cardstock. Add pen details. Mat auxiliary photos on second page in similar manner. Mount diagonally. Add a journaling block.

ONE Use a gridded ruler to draw a line all the way around a 12 x 12" piece of cardstock. The line should be ¼" from the outer edge of the page.

TWO To create a slanted black-and-white border, hold a template at a 35 degree angle to line and mark slanted parallel lines around all sides of the paper. Place a pencil dot on every other square in the pattern to aid in weaving.

THREE Cut along the slanted lines, stopping short of the main guideline on the page.

FOUR Cut four ¼ x 12" strips of white cardstock. Using the dotted squares along the edge as a guide, weave a strip along each side in an over-under pattern. Secure strips in each corner with adhesive. Turn over the assembly. The marked side is the back of the layout.

It was such fun to watch the change in your attitude when I brought out the camera and started taking these pictures. It took about three shots to change your "hat-titude" from grumpy to smiling and happy.

Jodi Amidei, Memory Makers

Hat-titudes

Make this mat and page decoration using a decorative ruler and a craft knife (see directions on adjacent page). Use those pieces you cut free for page decoration on a different page. Mat patterned paper over contrasting paper. Decorate with glitter glue. Mount the mat you have created on dark colored cardstock and add glitter glue. Tear a strip of patterned paper and place it across the top of the page. Embellish the torn edge with glitter glue. Double mat photos. Use letter stickers for a title and add a chalked vellum journaling block.

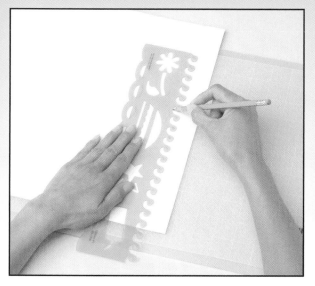 

ONE On the back side of a 12 x 12" piece of patterned paper, trace along the edge of a decorative ruler.

TWO Flip the ruler over and trace the edge again to create a mirror image of the first line. Cut out the shape with a craft knife. Remove the cut-out shape.

Bessie Logan Sparks
1884-1958
Mother of Alberta Sparks Danley

Valerie Barton, Flowood, Mississippi

Bessie Logan Sparks

Use a decorative template with double-sided patterned paper to make this lovely heritage page. Cut two 1 x 12" strips for the border using the decorative edge of a template. Adhere patterned strips facing each other on a 2½ x 12" piece of cardstock. Mat photo and place it on a large rectangular piece of paper. Add patterned paper strips to the top and bottom of the rectangular sheet. Add punched embellishments. Adhere a journaling block, fiber and small ribbon flowers. "Age" the fabric and journaling block by chalking edges.

Additional Page Instructions

Bookplate

Page 3–Torrey Miller, Thornton, Colorado

Although we used this artwork as a bookplate, it can be adapted very easily as a background for scrapbooking. Use the same technique with polymer clay and brass stencils as outlined on page 68 in Garden Party. Before baking clay, cut shape apart into five pieces. The interesting color was obtained by slightly overcooking clay on an aluminum baking sheet in a toaster oven. It was a happy "accident." Place mesh along the left side of page. Tie several different coordinating fibers together and adhere them across bottom of layout. Place clay pieces on foam dots and adhere over fibers to background. Title block is chalked torn cardstock mounted on foam squares to background. Entire page is then matted.

Rain

Page 6–Michele Gerbrandt, Memory Makers

Use the same technique as "Daddy's Girl" on page 38 to create the fun frames for this layout. Add glitter details to raindrops on frames and mat frame on white cardstock. String beads on wire and twist two strands together to make each of the bead accents. Adhere to background with glue dots. Cut out die cut title. Apply clear micro beads over letters in title and add glitter to highlight. Stick to background using foam dots. Mat background paper on contrasting color, and add torn strips of patterned paper top and bottom.

Camel Ride

Page 12–Jennifer Cain, Highlands Ranch, Colorado

Create a woven/layered border very easily with decorative scissors. Cut eight 8½ x 12" strips of cardstock using paper trimmer. Cut eight shorter strips of cardstock only this time cut one long edge on each strip with decorative scissors to add texture. Partially weave long vertical strips with short horizontal strips along right edge of layout. Double mat photos and add handmade photo corners using same decorative scissors. Embellish page with interesting metal accents. Attach journaling tags to photos with fiber. Stamp vellum tags for journaling and frame small photo with one of the tags. Add main printed journaling block to complete.

The Cabin

Page 12–Kelli Noto, Centennial, Colorado

The rustic pattern seen on this page was inspired by a Native American blanket and was created using two sizes of decorative pinking-edged scissors. To create this effect, cut along both sides of the long edges of cardstock strips. Alternate between mirror cuts (lining up the scissors to oppose the first cut exactly) and shadow cuts (lining up the scissors so they bite into the design of the first cut, repeating the first cut's design to create a rickrack effect). When the strips are adhered to the page, the negative spaces become part of the overall design. Mat photos and add punched title and trees. Mount diamond shapes cut from cardstock on self-adhesive foam spacers to complete the effect.

Scatter Joy

Page 40–Torrey Miller, Thornton, Colorado

A heart becomes a butterfly with the help of a Fiskar's shapecutter. To create the butterfly-shaped journaling windows, use the shapecutter on blue background to cut out mirrored hearts (overlapped in the middle with their points facing toward center). Leave a small section in the middle uncut on which to adhere the top wings. Use the same technique to cut the top wings out of vellum. Hand cut a cardstock frame and adhere over the vellum wings. Adhere center section of top wings to background with tacky tape for added strength. Cut butterfly bodies out of cardstock, cover in tacky tape, and coat with microbeads. Form wire antennae by hand and wrap bodies in wire. Adorn vellum wings with stickers, rhinestones and glitter. Print journaling on colored cardstock in various fonts and strategically place behind the butterfly-shaped windows on the background so that the journaling shows through the window. Adhere journaling to back of page. The top wings lift to reveal the journaling underneath. Embellish page with stickers and rhinestones. Die cut the title from cardstock and adhere. Mat page on cardstock.

Nature's Canyon

Page 66–Jodi Amidei, Memory Makers
Photos, Cheryl Banner, Arvada, Colorado

The stunning tile frame was created with polymer clay using the same technique as described in "Garden Party" on page 68. To "age" tiles, rub with brown dye-based ink after they're baked. Place photo on background and surround with tiles. Make the foreground of page by adhering a 12 x 10" piece of patterned paper to foam core board. Cut window in paper/foam core to a size that will reveal photo underneath. Add torn cardstock and fiber borders top and bottom. Attach secondary photos. Print out nature-related sayings onto transparency film. Cut apart and secure to page with brads.

Supply List for Pages

pg 3 Bookplate
Polymer clay (Sculpey), brass stencil (Heritage Handcrafts), patterned paper (Karen Foster Design), fibers (EK Success, On The Surface), mesh (Magic Mesh by Avant Card), cardstock (grey, mint), self-adhesive foam spacers, adhesive, glue dots, chalk.

pg 6 Rain
Teardrop punch (EK Success), letter die cuts (Sizzix), patterned paper (Paper Adventures), micro beads and colored beads (Halcraft), Sparkle diamond glitter glue (PSX Design), cardstock (aqua, white), wire, glue dots, self-adhesive foam spacers, craft knife, adhesive.

pg 12 The Cabin
Decorative scissors (Maxi Cuts, Family Treasures), tree punch (Carl), letter punches (Family Treasures), cardstock (oatmeal, forest green, burgundy, brown, taupe), adhesive.

pg 12 Camel Ride
Deckle scissors (Fiskars), letter stamp (Hero Arts), sun paper clip and camel bookmark (Pier One Imports), fibers (On The Surface), metal-rimmed vellum tags (Making Memories), cardstock (dark brown, red, evergreen, caramel), eyelets, adhesive.

pg 14 Scootin' Along
Personal Paper Trimmer (Fiskars), 2-sided mulberry paper (Pulsar Paper Products), letter stickers (Mrs. Grossman's Paper Co.), fibers (Cardladies.com), metal nameplate (Magic Scraps), mirrors (JewelCraft), metal-rimmed tag (Impress Rubber Stamps), eyelets, brads, chalk, vellum, cardstock (aqua, white), adhesive.

pg 15 Girls Just Wanna Have FUN
Personal Paper Trimmer (Fiskars), Flavia patterned paper (Colorbök), double-sided patterned paper (Daisy D's), metal-rimmed vellum tags (Making Memories), fiber (Fibers By The Yard), Jolees By You flower button stickers (EK Success), flower-shaped brads, vellum, chalk, cardstock (aqua), felt pen, adhesive.

pg 16 Wild Wild West
Personal Paper Trimmer (Fiskars), letter stamps (Stampin' Up!), cardstock (brown, maroon, navy, gray, yellow, tan), felt pen, adhesive.

pg 17 Alone We Can Do So Little…
Personal Paper Trimmer (Fiskars), letter stamps (Stampin' Up!), cardstock (black, lavender, sage green, white), felt pen, adhesive.

pg 18 Daniel Ryan
Personal Paper Trimmer with scoring blade (Fiskars), patterned paper (Frances Meyer), leaf laser die cut (Deluxe Designs), star brads (Magic Scraps), vellum, photo tape, felt pen, ruler, adhesive.

pg 19 Hula-Little Grass Shack
Personal Paper Trimmer (Fiskars), Patterned paper (Karen Foster Design), flower punches (Family Treasures), letter stamps (All Night Media), cardstock (orange, forest green, white, yellow, red), lettering template (Pebbles In My Pocket), clear UTEE (Suze Weinberg), fiber (Rubba Dub Dub), dark green stamping ink, adhesive

pg 20 Scarface
Personal Paper Trimmer (Fiskars), patterned paper (Rocky Mountain Scrapbook Co.), letter stickers (Making Memories), cardstock (beige, olive green), self-adhesive foam spacers, vellum, chalk, adhesive.

pg 22 Father
Red plaid patterned paper, metal letters, square brads, and metal photo corners (Making Memories), fibers (Rub A Dub Dub), blue patterned paper (EK Success), cardstock (burgundy, federal blue, white), adhesive.

pg 23 Miracle
Personal Paper Trimmer with perforating blade (Fiskars), fiber (EK Success), metal eyelet letters (Making Memories), vellum, brads, cardstock (eggplant, cream), 3-D metal heart charms (source unknown), adhesive.

pg 24 View of Two
Decorative scissors (Fiskars), Sonja die cut letters (QuickKutz), gold UTEE (Suze Weinberg), heat gun, tweezers, ribbon, cardstock (cranberry, evergreen, caramel), gold paint pen, felt pen, adhesive.

pg 25 Renaissance Festival
Decorative scissors (Fiskars), cardstock (oatmeal, powder blue), chalk, gold embossing powder, heat gun, adhesive.

pg 26 The Harris Family
Decorative scallop scissors (Creative Memories), oval cutting system (Creative Memories), vellum, cardstock (wisteria, royal purple), gold thread, adhesive.

pg 27 Rain
Decorative scissors (Fiskars), clear shrink film (K & B Innovations, Inc), die-cut letters (Sizzix), mesh (Magic Mesh by Avant Card), colored pencils, wire, silver jump rings, cardstock (granite, navy, Christmas red), navy stamping ink, self-adhesive foam spacers, adhesive.

pg 27 Keychains
Decorative scissors (Fiskars), clear shrink film (K & B Innovations, Inc.), colored pencils, ball chain.

pg 28 Azaleas
Decorative scissors (Fiskars), metallic thread (DMC), vellum, cardstock (hot pink, black), brads, adhesive.

pg 29 Spirograph
Decorative scissors (Fiskars, Provo Craft), wire, tiny eyelets, fibers (Rubba Dub Dub), cardstock (federal blue, turquoise, white, royal purple), self-adhesive foam spacers, adhesive.

pg 30 Winter Walk
Decorative scissors (Fiskars), fiber (On The Surface), die-cut letters (QuickKutz), cardstock (navy, bluegray, white), Sparkles diamond glitter (PSX Design), opaque white paint pen, adhesive.

pg 31 Bloom Where You're Planted
Decorative scissors (Fiskars), yellow patterned paper (Bo Bunny Press), blue patterned paper (Creative Imaginations), tag punch (EK Success), fiber (Gotyarn.com), wire, felt pen, self-adhesive foam spacers , mulberry paper, adhesive.

pg 32 Maine Summer Memories
Rubber stamps (Martha By Mail), ribbon, Versamark ink (Tsukineko), cardstock (light and dark green, lavender, deep purple, white faux botanical), chalk, pressed leaves/flowers (Pressed Petals, Inc.), acetate sheet, adhesive, felt pens, craft knife.

pg 34 Dance, Play, Smile…Dream
Fibers (EK Success, Making Memories, On The Surface), metal corners, eyelet letters and words (Making Memories), metal charms (Global Solutions), patterned paper (Karen Foster Design), plastic watch crystals (Deluxe),. mesh (Magic Mesh by Avant Card), cardstock (dark green, white), self-adhesive foam spacers, adhesive, glue dots, craft knife, tapestry needle.

Pg 35 Path To The Sea
Fibers (EK Success, On The Surface), ruler, craft knife, cardstock (royal purple, teal, celery), found objects, eyelets, adhesive.

Pg 36 Where The Buffalo Roam
Cardstock (black, oatmeal), self-adhesive foam spacers, felt pen, adhesive, craft knife.

pg 37 Estes Park
Metal letters (Making Memories), stickers (Colorbök), fiber (EK Success), metal butterfly and dragonfly (Darice), metallic thread, cardstock (buckeye, buttercup, cream), chalk, fine detail pen, adhesive, decorative brads.

Pg 38 Daddy's Girl
Leaf punch (Nankong), patterned paper and Sonnets letter stickers (Creative Imaginations), fiber (On The Surface), clear micro beads (Halcraft), cardstock (eggplant), brads, tacky tape, adhesive, craft knife, ruler.

pg 40 Scatter Joy
Heart template (Fiskars), vellum stickers (Stickopotamus), die-cut letters (QuickKutz), rhinestones (JewelCraft), Sparkle diamond glitter glue (PSX Design), clear micro beads (Magic Scraps), tape (Art Accents), wire, self-adhesive foam spacers, colored vellum (pink, buff, spring green), cardstock (navy, bright blue, buttercup, pastel green, dusty pink, canary yellow, bubble gum pink, dark pink, celery, peach, white), craft knife, adhesive.

pg 42 How Suite It Is
Circle Scissor (EK Success), fibers (Fibers By The Yard), letter stickers (Doodlebug Design), tagboard tags (DMD), cardstock (burgundy, black, light brown), craft knife, adhesive, felt pen.

Supply List for Pages *(continued)*

pg 42 It Is a Happy Talent…
Circle template (Provo Craft), cardstock (pumpkin, cream), craft knife, adhesive.

pg 43 Austin
Circle cropper (Making Memories), lettering template (EK Success), patterned paper (Colorbok), number stamps (Hero Arts), opaque lavender stamping ink, colored pencils, cardstock (purple, white), felt pen, adhesive.

pg 44 Brinley
Circle and Oval cutting system (Creative Memories), patterned paper (Design Originals), punches (EK Success), fibers (Rubba Dub Dub), metal tag (FoofaLa), paper yarn (Making Memories), Suede (Crafter's Workshop), metal impact stamps (FoofaLa), clear and copper UTEE (Suze Weinberg), stamps (All Night Media, Hampton Art, Raindrops on Roses), patterned cardstock (Family Treasures), cardstock (green, white, caramel), brads, texturizing paste, walnut ink (Anima Designs), eyelets, sewing machine, adhesive, self-adhesive foam spacers.

pg 45 Don't Judge Each Day…(envelope)
Circle Scissor (EK Success), flower die cut (EK Success), vellum, cardstock (chili, rusty brown, caramel), fiber (EK Success), eyelets, self-adhesive foam spacers, seeds, heart punch (EK Success), adhesive.

pg 46 Tom and Jodi
Heart template (Provo Craft), patterned paper (Daisy D's), letter stickers (Stickopotamus), gold micro beads (Art Accents), vellum, adhesive, craft knife.

pg 47 Moonlight Dreams
Circle cutting system (Creative Memories), sparkle diamond glitter glue (PSX Design), border stickers (Mrs. Grossman's Paper Co.), silk bridal floral spray (Michael's), cardstock (cream parchment, pink parchment), adhesive.

pg 48 Prom Memories
Circle Scissor (EK Success), Marisa die-cut letters (QuicKutz), square metal brads (Creative Impressions), rose photo corners (EK Success), colored pencils (red, silver), metallic paper (red, silver), cardstock (black, white), self-adhesive foam spacers, adhesive, ribbon roses.

pg 49 So Cozy
Circle scissor (EK Success), patterned paper (Bo Bunny Press, Colors By Design), letter stickers (Bo Bunny Press), stickers (Mrs. Grossman's Paper Co.), watercolor pencils (Staedtler), white cardstock, adhesive, felt pen.

pg 50 Bodie Island Lighthouse
Shapecutter template (Fiskars), decorative scissors (Fiskars), stamp (PSX Design), printed vellum (Fiskars), cardstock (yellow, turquoise, white, black), blue stamping ink, adhesive.

pg 51 Sisters Are Forever Friends
Heart border punch and shape cutter (Fiskars), patterned paper and patterned vellum (Fiskars), cardstock (white, strawberry, Christmas red), brads, vellum, adhesive.

pg 52 Jordan Kennedy
Punch (Punch Bunch), patterned paper (Karen Foster Design), mesh (Magic Mesh by Avant Card), tape (Art Accents), clear micro beads (Halcraft), brads, printable transparency film, stamping ink, white cardstock, dauber for applying ink, adhesive.

pg 53 What a Clown
Embroidery floss (DMC), standard hole punch (Office Max), 1/16" hole punch (Family Treasures), cardstock (pink, turquoise, yellow, cream), large-eyed needle, pearl bead, adhesive, felt pens.

pg 54 The Giant Snowman
Snowman, snowflake, and doll-clothes die cuts (Accu-Cut), buttons (Jesse James, Magic Scraps), patterned paper (Bo Bunny Press, Creative Imaginations), shaved ice glitter (Magic Scraps), foam core paper, brads, beads, wire, vellum, acetate sheet, cardstock (royal blue, brown, white), adhesive.

pg 55 Sun Kissed
Punches (EK Success), Ek-streme Edges border strip (EK Success), stickers (EK Success), cardstock (pumpkin, bright blue, oatmeal), foam tape, beads, adhesive.

pg 56 Camp Hop
Frog die cut (Sizzix), letter template (C-Thru Ruler Co.), patterned paper (EK Success), anywhere hole punch, brads, vellum, cardstock (dark green, yellow), fibers, beads, adhesive, craft knife, embossing powder, heat gun, embossing ink, felt pen.

pg 57 These Boots Were Made for Walking
Paper doll die cut (Sizzix), metal flowers and brads (Making Memories), punch (Family Treasures), adhesed foil, black pen, chain, vellum, patterned paper (Doodlebug Design), black embossing powder, cardstock, heat gun, adhesive, anywhere hole punch.

pg 58 Children Are God's Way…
Heart die cut die (Ellison), patterned paper and rubber stamp (Magenta), Versamark ink (Tsukineko), beads (Magic Scraps), cardstock (spearmint, cranberry, burgundy), beads, wire, self-adhesive foam tape, adhesive.

pg 59 Flowers
Straight and wavy weaving die cuts (Dayco), flower die cut (Create-A-Cut), copper letters (Global Solutions), wire, self-adhesive foam spacers, cardstock (hemlock, evergreen, pumpkin, orange, red-orange, buttercup, white), patterned paper (Provo Craft), adhesive. Xyron machine.

pg 60 Photo Shoot
Dragonfly die cuts (Sizzix), patterned paper (Creative Imaginations), wire mesh (Paragona), fun foam, clear shrink plastic (Lucky Squirrel), Pearl-Ex pigment powder (Jacquard Products), Versamark ink (Tsukineko), metal-rimmed vellum tag (Creative Imaginations), fiber (Gotyarn.com), rubber stamps (Limited Edition, 200 Plus), vellum, cardstock (cactus, pale mint), self-adhesive foam spacers, adhesive, glue dots.

pg 61 Coming Home To Tennessee
Die-cut letters and shapes (Sizzix), patterned paper, polymer letter tiles, and letter stickers (Sweetwater), Fibers (EK Success), metal eyelet letters (Making Memories), copper metal sheet (Paragona), cork, burlap, stamping ink, mulberry paper, aluminum foil, heart brads (Creative Impressions), hemp, eyelets, vellum, adhesive, corrugated paper, gold metallic paper, chalk.

pg 62 Our Fall Wedding
Leaf die cuts (Sizzix), colored vellum (red, orange, maroon, white), brads, cardstock (maroon, orange, golden yellow, purple, craft paper, black), adhesive.

pg 63 Michigan Lakes
#3 Spiral die (Accu-Cut), Grande Mark Roller Die Cutting Machine (Accu-Cut), patterned cardstock (Crafter's Workshop), cardstock (black, two-tone gray), vellum, brads, adhesive.

pg 64 Hoppy Easter
Bunny die cut (Sizzix), patterned paper (Keeping Memories Alive), cardstock (periwinkle, caramel, beige, pink, black), letter stickers (Making Memories), adhesive, felt pen, self-adhesive foam spacers.

pg 65 Pumpkin Princess
Patterned paper (Provo Craft), Fall & Halloween templates (Provo Craft), sparkly tulle, gold twine, brads, cardstock (ivory, buckeye), gold metallic thread, sewing machine, adhesive.

pg 66 Nature's Canyon
Polymer clay (Sculpey), brass stencils (Lasting Impressions), fibers (Rub A Dub Dub), patterned paper (Fiskars), printable transparency film, brads, cardstock (evergreen, rust, white), brown stamping ink, foam core paper, adhesive, craft knife.

pg 68 Garden Party
Polymer clay (Sculpey), brass stencils (Lasting Impressions), fibers (Club Scrap, Funky Fringes Lions Brand, On The Surface), Preserve-It matte acrylic sealant (Krylon), cardstock (holly, rust, pumpkin, white), adhesive, craft knife, sandpaper or emery board, chalk.

pg 69 Celebrate
Polymer clay (Sculpey), "Celebrate" brass stencil (Plane Class), metallic mesh (Robin's Nest), patterned paper (Paper Adventures), silver leafing pen (Krylon), star brads (Creative Impressions), spiral clips (Target Stores, Inc.), glue dots, silver metallic paper, adhesive, craft knife, silver floss.

pg 70 Winter White
101 Crackle paste (US Art Quest), brass stencil (Heritage Handcrafts), patterned paper (Scrappin' Dreams), metal-rimmed vellum tag (Making Memories), letter stickers (Making Memories), alphabet beads (Darice), fibers (Cut-It-Up), organza ribbon (Jo-Ann Fabrics), vellum, adhesive, ribbon, cardstock (white, blue).

pg. 71 Lessons Learned From a Lime Green Cast
Lettering template (Frances Meyer), crackle paste (US Art Quest), rubber stamps (Hero Arts), patterned paper (Provo Craft), metal-rimmed vellum tag (Making Memories), stamping ink, gauze mesh, vellum, cardstock (celery, lime green), flower shaped brads, adhesive.

pg 72 Surely a Star Danced…
Rectangle template (Provo Craft), acrylic paint (Synta, Inc), Chinese coins, cream cardstock, paint brush, adhesive.

pg 73 Cousins
Rectangle template (Provo Craft), rubber stamp and ink (Stampin' Up), fibers (On The Surface), cardstock (celery, cactus), adhesive.

pg 73 Ya Ya Sisterhood
"Whimsy" Lettering template (Scrap Pagerz), hat brass stencil (Lasting Impressions), printed paper (Club Scrap), paper yarn (Making Memories), texturizing paste (Dreamweaver), pave pearl accents, scalloped scissors, cardstock (peacock blue, olive green, plum, black), purple and blue embossing powders, eyelets, adhesive, felt pen.

pg 74 Sun Goddess
Brass stencil (T.S.C. Designs), fibers (EK Success), raffia ribbon (Gallery), brass sun charm (source unknown), cardstock (dark brown, craft paper, cream, ivory), chalk, stamping ink, sewing machine, adhesive, self-adhesive foam spacers.

pg 75 Love Letter
Fancy Caps lettering template (Wordsworth), border sticker (K & Company), metal-rimmed tag (Avery), butterfly charm (source unknown), white gel pen, chalk, cardstock (purple, white), adhesive, felt pen.

pg 75 Reading Is Pure Dead Brilliant
"Mini Charmed Letters" lettering template (Crafter's Workshop), metal eyelet letters (Making Memories), silver gel pen, cardstock (black, Christmas red, violet, teal), vellum, brads, silver embossing powder, embossing ink, heat gun, adhesive.

pg 76 United in Love
Shape template (EK Success), oval cutting system (Creative Memories), circle punch (Carl), colored vellum (hunter, cranberry, pink, white), black cardstock, stylus, gold gel pen, felt pen, adhesive.

pg 77 Lazy Days of Summer
Lettering template (Provo Craft), Alphabet template (Accu-Cut), circle cutting system template (Creative Memories), Xyron machine, cardstock (sparkly blue-gray), stylus, felt pens, white gel pen, adhesive.

pg 78 Help! I'm Being Eaten
Lettering template (Scrap Pagerz), jewelry findings (Darice), memorabilia pocket (3L), cardstock (black, celery, army green, brown, ginger), felt pen, eyelets, adhesive.

pg 79 Summertime and the Living Is Easy
Patterned paper (PrintWorks, Pebbles In My Pocket), paper yarn (Making Memories), decorative eyelets, sun sticker (source unknown), self-adhesive foam spacers, adhesive, felt pen.

pg 80 Grandma Karen's First Grade Class
Shape and circle templates (Provo Craft), patterned paper (Provo Craft), Art Emboss medium-weight metal sheets (Paragona), embroidery floss (DMC), black cardstock, vellum, eyelets, adhesive, stylus.

pg 81 "JD"
Letter template (C-Thru Ruler), pre-cut blue offset window cardstock (C-Thru Ruler), metal sheet (Paragona), patterned paper (Keeping Memories Alive), stylus, deckle scissors (Fiskars), silver paper, cardstock (black, ivory), adhesive, felt pen, self-adhesive foam spacers.

Page 81 Nativity Card
Brass stencil (Heritage Handcrafts), Art Emboss medium-weight metal sheet (Paragona), deckle scissors (Fiskars), black cardstock, self-adhesive foam spacers.

pg 82 Heart Strings
Letter and primitive heart templates (Provo Craft), fiber (Magic Scraps), patterned paper (Provo Craft), mulberry paper (Magenta), vellum, brads, buttons, mesh fabric (source unknown), white cardstock, adhesive.

pg 83 Sorting Hearts
Primitive heart template (Provo Craft), patterned paper (Provo Craft), decorative eyelets, brads, red mesh (Magic Mesh by Avant Card), chalk, letter stamps (Hero Arts), stamping ink, date stamp (source unknown), cardstock (white, oatmeal), self-adhesive foam spacers, adhesive, embroidery floss (DMC), felt pen.

pg 83 Wind Cave
Lettering stencil, Alphabitties letter stickers, and patterned paper (Provo Craft), letter stamps (Hero Arts, PSX Design), chalk, fibers (On The Surface), cardstock (brown, red, black), vellum, stamping ink, eyelets, felt pen, adhesive.

pg 84 Fall
Celebrations template (Fiskars), punches (Fiskars, Punch Bunch), leaf stamp (PSX Design), Versamark ink (Tsukineko), cardstock (pumpkin, burnt orange, evergreen, ivory), adhesives, lettering template (source unknown).

pg 85 Never Lose Your Joy
Decorative ruler (C-Thru Ruler), cardstock (aqua, periwinkle, white, blue-gray), vellum, felt pen, adhesive.

pg 86 Colorado
Decorative ruler (Cut-It-Up), gold micro beads (Art Accents), leaf studs (JewelCraft), journaling sticker and letter rubber stamps (Wordsworth), fiber (Rubba Dub Dub), silk ribbon, pale yellow embroidery floss, vellum, cardstock (white, black, buttercup), tacky tape, piercing tool, adhesive.

pg 87 First Time Grandma
Decorative ruler (Creative Memories), patterned paper (Patchwork Design, Inc.), alphabet beads (Westrim), foil photo corners (3L), flower punch (EK Success), variegated fiber (On The Surface), vellum (white, pink), ribbon (Offray), decorative eyelets, adhesive, rhinestones (Stampa Rosa).

pg 87 Friends
Letter template (EK Success), brass flower template (Lasting Impressions), embroidery floss (DMC), cardstock (ivory, sage, blush), felt pen, adhesive.

pg 88 Four Wheelin'
Border template (EK Success), craft knife, cardstock (deep red, black, white), white gel pen, adhesive, black felt pen.

pg 90 Hat-titudes
Decorative ruler (C-Thru Ruler), patterned paper (NRN Designs, Two Busy Moms), sticker letters (Creative Imaginations), Sparkles diamond glitter glue (PSX Design), cardstock (white, dark purple), chalk, vellum, felt pen, adhesive, craft knife.

pg 91 Bessie Logan Sparks
Border Buddy (EK Success), fibers (Fibers By The Yard), double-sided patterned paper (Daisy D's), ribbon flowers (Offray), punch (EK Success), cardstock (caramel, beige), chalk, adhesive.

The following companies contributed artwork towards this book:

Accu-Cut® (wholesale only)
(800) 288-1670
www.accucut.com

C-Thru® Ruler Company, The (wholesale only)
(800) 243-8419
www.cthruruler.com

EK Success™ Ltd. (wholesale only)
(800) 524-1359
www.eksuccess.com

Ellison® Craft and Design
(800) 253-2238
www.ellison.com

Fiskars, Inc. (wholesale only)
(715) 842-2091
www.fiskars.com

Heritage Handcrafts
(303) 683-0963

Provo Craft®
(888) 577-3545
www.provocraft.com

Index